T0286586

Buddhism for Busy People

Buddhism *for* Busy People

Finding Happiness in a Hurried World

David Michie

SHAMBHALA
BOULDER
2017

Shambhala Publications, Inc.
4720 Walnut Street
Boulder, Colorado 80301
www.shambhala.com

9 8 7 6 5 4 3 2 1

Printed in the United States of America

♾ This edition is printed on acid-free paper that meets the
American National Standards Institute z39.48 Standard.
♻ This book is printed on 30% postconsumer recycled paper.
For more information please visit www.shambhala.com.
Distributed in the United States by Penguin Random House LLC
and in Canada by Random House of Canada Ltd

The Library of Congress catalogues the previous edition of this book as follows:
Michie, David.
Buddhism for busy people: finding happiness in an
uncertain world / David Michie.
p. cm.
Previously published: Crows Nest, Australia:
Allen & Unwin, 2004.
Includes bibliographical references and index.
ISBN 978-1-55939-298-3 (Snow Lion edition)
ISBN 978-1-61180-367-9 (Shambhala edition)
1. Religious life—Buddhism. 2. Buddhism—Doctrines.
3. Happiness—religious aspects—Buddhism. I. Title.
BQ5405.M53 2004
294.3'444—dc22
2008001961

Dedication

THIS BOOK IS DEDICATED with heartfelt gratitude to my dharma teachers: Geshe Acharya Thubten Loden, founder of the Tibetan Buddhist Society, and Les Sheehy, director of the Tibetan Buddhist Society in Perth, Western Australia, whose kindness I can never repay, and without whom this book could never have been written.

Contents

Acknowledgments

I GRATEFULLY ACKNOWLEDGE Geshe Acharya Thubten Loden from whose comprehensive book *Path to Enlightenment in Tibetan Buddhism* (Melbourne: Tushita Publications, 1993) I have drawn many of the translated verses of Shantideva's great classic *Bodhicharyavatara*.

I would also like to acknowledge H.H. the Dalai Lama's *The Path to Enlightenment*, edited and translated by Glenn H. Mullin (Ithaca, N.Y.: Snow Lion Publications, 1995), from which I have sourced direct commentary by His Holiness.

Introduction to the 2017 Edition

TWELVE YEARS AFTER *Buddhism for Busy People* was first published, I am delighted by the way the book continues to resonate with readers around the world. I regularly receive heartwarming messages from people telling me what the book has meant to them. Some even share ways in which they decided to change elements of their lives—large or small—after reading the book.

One middle-aged man picked up the phone to call his sister from whom he had been estranged for many years, leading to a family reconciliation. A young woman found the courage she needed to open a shop selling inspirational books and self-development programs. Then there was the couple who threw out high-flying corporate jobs to create an animal sanctuary.

I suggest none of these things in this book, and I certainly claim no credit for the brave and transformational decisions of others. What they illuminate, however, are the ways in which the practices first offered by Buddha two and a half thousand years ago still have a direct and powerful relevance to us today. Exactly how they may impact each one of us is part of an unfolding journey of discovery—one that grows all the more life-enhancing with each passing year.

Both the title and subtitle of this book were chosen to reflect the zeitgeist of the early years of this century. Mobile phones and the Internet had recently become ubiquitous. We had just lived through the bursting of the dot-com bubble and the 9/11 attacks. Scientists started talking about climate change. Many of the reassuring certainties of life seemed to be dissolving beneath our feet. We had never felt busier.

Fast forward to the present, and the pace of life back in the early 2000s seems positively quaint. Life before Facebook? Mobile phones that weren't online? What do you mean you didn't check the sales spreadsheet before you came into work this morning—I forwarded them to you last night?!

The convergence of mobile technology and the Internet has fundamentally changed society, as we can observe at a glance on any city street, railway carriage, or school yard. Along with the demands of the real world, a global, twenty-four–hour virtual world has insinuated itself into many people's lives with compelling potency.

While there is no doubt that we have taken a giant leap forward in connectivity, access to information, and a myriad other ways, all this has come at a cost. A growing body of research shows that high usage of social media degrades our attention spans. We are less able to recall things and are more easily distracted. A recent study showed that the average teenager checks his or her social media one hundred times a day. Fear of Missing Out (FoMO) and the need to project an often impossibly enviable version of oneself online has piled a new set of pressures onto those of an age when trying to arrive at a resolved, adult identity is fraught enough. Is it any wonder that anxiety among teenagers is at sky-high levels?

Even those of us who should know better sometimes find it

hard to avoid the siren calls of social media. Sitting to meditate, reading a mind-improving book or even a blog is something we may promise ourselves we fully intend to do . . . after we have checked our social media feed. It's hard to ignore the paradox that, at a time in history when it's never been easier to access the spiritual wisdom—for millennia the preserve of an elite few—we have never been less interested or mentally capable of using it!

The digital revolution has been one of the game changers of the past decade, ramping up our busyness and sense of volatility. But it hasn't been the only one. The Global Financial Crisis has been an earthquake inflicting massive damage on whole industries and communities, which continues to reverberate around the world today. September 11 set off a chain of events leading to the rise of a new breed of do-it-yourself terror groups, bringing the prospect of violent and random massacres of ordinary people into our own cities. And evidence of climate change suggests that extreme and unseasonal weather patterns are now part of our new normal.

Fortunately for those with an interest in a permanent solution to well-being, none of these developments need be as worrisome as they may appear. In fact, there is nothing quite like a sense of deep disillusionment with conventional reality to prompt us to ask the questions that really matter. Questions like: Is there an enduring source of happiness I can rely on through all this frenetic activity and upheaval? If I can't change reality, can I at least change the way I experience it? Who, really, is this person called "me," and is there any point to my life besides enjoying whatever pleasures I can find along the way?

The reason that Buddha's teachings have continued to be handed down to us through the centuries is because they offer such exciting, radical, and perspective-shifting insights. While those insights haven't changed, what has changed, particularly in recent years, are the advances made by scientists, which have brought about a fascinating convergence of East and West, ancient and contemporary.

Yes, cognitive therapists now confirm, it is not events in the outside world that make us feel elated or miserable, but the way we interpret them. Medical researchers are now able to attest to the significant, holistic, multifactorial range of benefits delivered by meditation, not least being the capacity to shift our "set point" for happiness. Neurobiologists can certainly confirm that what we see, hear, and perceive of the outside world is not so much what is "out there" as it is a projection of our minds. And quantum scientists use almost identical language as Buddha himself to describe the ultimate nature of reality as well as our relationship with it.

When we live our lives in accordance with the way that things really are, rather than with some baseless negative narrative, we are very much more likely to operate more effectively, both for our own benefit as well as for those around us. When we catch a glimpse of our own true nature beneath the surface agitation, discovering ourselves as beings of boundless radiance, tranquillity, and benevolence, we begin to awaken to what is real and enduring. A state of being that supports equanimity in the face of chaos, and calm amid a frenetic pace of life.

It is my sincere hope that readers of *Buddhism for Busy People* will continue to enjoy family reconciliations, fresh entrepreneurial adventures, the creation of animal sanctuaries, and many other wonders besides! More than this, it is my heartfelt wish that each one of you will discover in the wisdom of my kind and extraordinary teachers—for whom I am a mere conduit—that you really do possess Buddha nature. You may keep it well hidden—even from yourself!—but deep down you are a being of pure, great love and pure, great compassion. Come home to yourself, dear reader, and all is well.

Buddhism for Busy People

1. What Does It Take to Be Happy?

A poor man, Depa, once found an enormously valuable jewel.
Being a person of little desire, and content with his small income,
Depa pondered to whom he should give the jewel. He tried to
think who was most in need and suddenly was inspired to give
the jewel to King Prasenajit. The king was astounded as there
were many poor and needy people, but Depa said, "O King,"
it is you who is the poorest, because you lack contentment!"

——————— Nagarjuna, *Letter to a Friend* ———————

HAT DOES IT TAKE to be happy? Of all the questions in the world, this is the most universal. It is also the great leveler because all of us—comfortably off or financially struggling, single or in a relationship, awkwardly overweight or elegantly slim—are equal in our desire to achieve true happiness. Not the happiness we've all experienced which comes and goes depending on circumstance, but a happiness which endures regardless of change. A happiness we feel deep down inside.

By any objective standard, our efforts to attain this simple goal have met with decidedly mixed results. As a society we now enjoy a level of affluence that would have left our grandparents breathless—but our medicine cabinets have never been so replete with sedatives, tranquilizers, and antidepressants to cocoon us from our new, "improved" reality. We have at our disposal an unprecedented range of labor-saving devices—but never have we had to work such long hours. We are succeeding in the cozy notion of creating a "global village"—but never have we felt so under siege from international terrorism, volatile stock markets, viral infections, and other threats. And so the list of paradoxes continues.

On an individual basis, our striving for happy, purposeful lives often doesn't fare much better. Money, relationships, and fulfillment in work are the core ingredients of most people's recipes for happiness, but if we were to send in the Happiness Auditors to check up on their effectiveness, could they really withstand close scrutiny?

Successive studies of lottery winners, for example, show that within months of multimillion-dollar wins, happiness levels return pretty much to where they were before. Amazingly adaptable creatures that we are, we adjust to new conditions so quickly that what was once fabulous soon becomes the norm, and we're back where we started, in search of fresh excitement. Even when we do achieve that much sought-after promotion, that big-ticket deal, that amazing breakthrough, all too often we are mystified to discover that we fail to experience the wonderful feelings we'd always thought we would. "Is this all?," we find ourselves wondering.

And in our relationships, we don't have to look very far to recognize just how swiftly and how often that first giddying rush of romantic intensity can turn into something quite different.

Yet somehow we manage to convince ourselves that it's not

the recipe that's at fault—it's the ingredients we're working with. If only we were to land *this* particular job or contract, the difference would be life changing. *That* man or woman is just so right that life with them would transport us to a state of great bliss. The fact that we once entertained similar thoughts about our now very-ex partner is not a subject we like to think about. And if we do, we have an outstanding ability to convince ourselves that this time it will all be completely different!

A practical alternative

Having spent my adult life in corporate public relations, my own search for happiness has been a busy one. On the career treadmill working crazy hours, juggling a dozen balls, experiencing the full spectrum of emotions from adrenaline-charged triumph to the desperate wish that the world would stop, I am all too familiar with the relentless striving to succeed, the wearying knowledge that no matter how far you go, there is always so much further.

But it has also been my enormous good fortune to have encountered Tibetan Buddhism, to have discovered a practical alternative. This book explains how profound and lasting happiness can be achieved according to this ancient tradition. It is also an unashamedly personal account of how Buddhist teachings have helped me infuse my day-to-day life with greater meaning and how they are transforming my understanding about what really counts.

Personal though this particular account may be, it is written with the certain knowledge that there is nothing at all unique about my experience. Scratch out corporate public relations and replace it with any other form of busy-ness and the story for most of us is a variation on the same theme: too much to do, too little time to do it in, and an underlying recognition that despite our best endeavors we don't appear to be living life to our full potential. It is also true that by integrating various Buddhist practices into my life, I have benefited from results which are by no means unique either—and still do, every single day.

If, like me, you have a tendency to take yourself altogether too seriously, beating yourself up when things don't go according to plan; if you feel your chances of happiness are undermined by circumstances beyond your control; if you would like to be a kinder, more generous person, but your heart has been cauterized by hurt and fear; if you would, quite simply, like to experience a sense of meaning beyond "another day, another dollar," you may well find in Buddhism practices which are truly transforming.

Rearranging not the externals, but the internals

What, you might ask, can a tradition developed in a remote oriental fiefdom two and a half thousand years ago possibly teach Westerners in the twenty-first century about happiness?

One of the most amazing paradoxes of all is that the Tibetan Buddhist approach could have been developed with today's busy Western world specifically in mind. In the finest empirical form, it presents an approach to the human condition based on an unflinching analysis of fact. It provides tried and tested practices set out in clearly defined steps to lead us from our current mental state to greater happiness and, ultimately, enlightenment.

From the Buddhist viewpoint, our attempts to rearrange the externals of our lives—money, relationships, careers—can only ever result in temporary satisfaction, the reason being that all such attempts fail to take into account the only constant in life: change. Even if we do get things the way we want them for a while, inevitably something will come along to upset our plans.

This doesn't mean we should give up on happiness but rather that we should adopt a more effective strategy to reach that state. The Buddhist sage Shantideva once gave an eloquent analogy:

> Where would I possibly find enough leather
> With which to cover the surface of the earth?
> But wearing leather just on the soles of my shoes
> Is equivalent to covering the earth with it.

In other words, instead of attempting the impossible task of trying to control our whole environment, the Buddhist philosophy is to take control of the way we *experience* that environment—in our minds. Our objective is to rearrange not the externals but the internals, to identify our habitual, negative patterns of thinking and replace them with more positive alternatives, to change not the world but the way we experience it.

"Which is all very well," you may be thinking, "but if you had to live/work/sleep with the children/boss/husband I do, no amount of mental gymnastics is going to change things."

So it may seem. But even in the most difficult circumstances, change is possible. It is for this very reason that one of the best recognized symbols of Buddhism is the lotus, a plant which, though rooted in the filth of the swamps, transcends its surroundings to rise to the surface as a flower of the most extraordinary beauty.

A practice-based psychology

How is such transcendence achieved? Not through hoping or wishing, but by engaging in well-established practices which for thousands of years have been shown to deliver successful results.

"What do Buddhists believe?" is a question often asked. Because belief lies at the heart of the Judeo-Christian tradition, the assumption is that Buddhism too is founded on belief and that Shakyamuni Buddha is the Buddhist equivalent of Jesus or Mohammed.

In fact, Buddhism works according to a completely different model. Buddhists do not worship Buddha; rather, we regard him as an example of what we can all achieve if we quite literally put our minds to it. Buddhism suggests no ultimate divinity who will make things better, but instead provides us with the mental software we need to make things better for ourselves—and, of course, others.

The subtitle of this book, "Finding happiness in an uncertain world," refers to a deliberate process. If we wish to learn the piano or improve our golf game, we know it isn't good enough simply to own the right equipment. We have to learn how to use it, step-by-step, practicing the relevant techniques until we achieve a level of mastery. So it is with our minds, where the effects of Buddhist practices are observable, repeatable and measurable.

A path of happiness

Where does one begin finding out about this path which is both ancient and advanced, practical and transcendent, radical and profoundly reassuring? Shakyamuni Buddha is said to have given eighty-four thousand teachings during his lifetime, but it is our very good fortune that the essence of these was distilled by Atisha, one of Buddhism's most important teachers, who took Buddhism from India to Tibet. Atisha's instructions are known as the *Lam Rim*, which translates approximately as "the Path to Enlightenment." Within Tibetan Buddhism there are a number of different schools, each with its own particular emphasis and terminology. While some attach greater importance to the Lam Rim as a text than others, the teachings contained within it are precious to them all.

Buddhism for Busy People provides an introduction to the core teachings of Buddhism. It does not pretend to be a comprehensive explanation, which is already available in a number of different books, including the superlative *Path to Enlightenment* by my own teacher, Geshe Acharya Thubten Loden. At this point it's also important to say that I am in no way claiming to be a "professional"—that is, a teacher, lama, or monk. It is for that very reason that I hope this book may be useful to the busy people it is aimed at—because I am a busy person too.

In telling my own story as a very typical busy person, outlining the Lam Rim teachings and how they help me, it is my heartfelt wish that you will find in this book something you can relate to, something of value. Perhaps some concepts or techniques will strike you as useful, while others may seem less so. And that's fine. Buddhism is very much more "à la carte" than "set menu." Take those practices which work for you as an individual, where you are now, and leave the others to one side.

Because this is a personal account, it involves real people. In order not to compromise their privacy I have changed some names. But rest assured, I have taken no fictional license with the Lam Rim.

Explaining Buddhist teachings, or the Dharma, as they are collectively known, is rather like trying to describe a richly embroidered tapestry in terms of the separate threads from which it is woven. The interrelationships are such that it's difficult to unravel one thread without referring to others. My hope is that whether you are completely new to Buddhism, or are already familiar with the Lam Rim, you may find in the teachings I quote fresh sources of illumination.

Enlightenment can seem a long way off—most of us can only guess at what it means. But the Lam Rim is also the path to happiness, and that's something we can understand better. Not the short-lived, worldly happiness we have all felt, and lost, so many times throughout our lives, but an enduring and heartfelt serenity, a sense of meaning which goes beyond narrow self-interest to encompass the well-being of all those around us, an experience of our ultimate nature as pristine, boundless and beyond death.

For it is Buddha's promise that, like the lotus, our destiny is a future radiance beyond anything we might presently conceive, as we rise above the swamp to achieve the supreme bliss of transcendence.

2. Buddha's First Teaching

THE FOUR NOBLE TRUTHS

Buddhas don't wash away sins with water,
Or heal suffering with laying on of hands,
Or transmit understanding into the minds of others.
They introduce beings to freedom
Through showing them reality.

MATERCHETA

ACCORDING TO CONVENTIONAL WISDOM, it is life's great tragedies that propel us to search for deeper meaning. Love lost, hopes dashed, career threatened with ruin—it is when such dark shadows fall upon our lives, so the theory goes, that we reach out for something more, something to explain what is happening to us or, at the very least, to provide us with a source of comfort. But like so much conventional wisdom, this is only part of the truth.

What happens when our careers and home life are in acceptable shape, but we are still feeling dissatisfied? When we enjoy, very much, the finer things in life, but are still faced in our more reflective moments with a nagging unease? In a world in which so many of our usual certainties are under threat, many of us live with an underlying sense of dislocation and futility.

In my own case, I came to Buddhism not because I'd reached rock bottom, but paradoxically because in worldly terms I was starting to do rather well. Living in London, I was upwardly mobile in my chosen career. The sumptuously appointed offices of the public relations consultancy where I worked had a commanding view over Trafalgar Square, so that I felt at the very heart of the capital. I was happily married, and we had a flat in the increasingly trendy area between Wandsworth and Clapham Commons. While I never took home the kinds of six-figure bonuses lavishly bestowed on my contemporaries in the City, neither did I feel poor. Smart restaurants, foreign travel, and luxury German cars were all part of my lifestyle.

Even as I write this, though, I can't escape the self-conscious recognition that the life I am describing sounds far more glamorous than it ever felt at the time. And that was the problem. Instead of being flushed with fulfillment at the realization of long-cherished dreams, far from being thrilled by the prospect of ascending the metaphorical career ladder, what I felt at that time, more than anything, was a sense of profound weariness. For my achievements, such as they were, came at a price.

The cost of success

Punishingly long hours, relentless deadlines, and the need to manage a constant succession of conflicting client demands made it hard to indulge in life's fleeting pleasures with any great joy. I regarded luxuries merely as compensation for the various trials I faced every day on the front line.

As time went on, this grinding lifestyle made it harder and

harder to experience very much in the way of relaxation or even simple hedonism. Worn down, anesthetized, I found that the specter of work overshadowed every experience. Terence Conran restaurants. Weekend jaunts to Prague. So what? Who cared? With three new business pitches in the next fortnight, not to mention a pack of clients remorseless in their demands, there was never any escaping the office. Somewhere between my bright-eyed youth and my mid-thirties, on a level I couldn't define, I seemed to have stopped living.

Worse still was the recognition that having made some strides towards my ambitions, the rewards were less spectacular than I'd anticipated. My pay looked all very well on paper—so why was it that I didn't feel rich? It seemed that a still larger income was required. But now, unlike my attitude in my earlier years in the industry, I realized that with more money would come still greater pressures. And was that what I really wanted? Like a hamster racing on a wheel, the faster I ran, the faster I would have to run.

Clambering my way to the top of PR's greasy pole had never really been foremost among my ambitions. In fact, from the age of eighteen through till about thirty-two I had been relentless in my pursuit of a career as an author. Instead of spending my twenties like most healthy young men, partying, womanizing, and generally misbehaving, I'd shut myself away at nights and over weekends writing novel after novel, approaching publisher after publisher in an increasingly feverish attempt to break into print. I had tried the whole gamut of possible genres, from *Boy's Own* adventures to commercial romance fiction before, ten unpublished manuscripts later, finally deciding to throw in the towel. My PR career had become so demanding I simply had no energy left for anything else.

But now I began to feel I lacked the energy for even that, especially when crammed into ludicrously overcrowded Underground carriages, or gridlocked in bumper-to-bumper traffic on the Embankment. Back at home on one of the bookshelves was a tome packed with compelling arguments for downshifting, but whatever way I looked at it I couldn't see myself throwing up my London base for an uncertain future somewhere else. The truth was that my skills and personality ideally suited me for the job. I liked what I did. I just didn't want to do so much of it.

The situation in which I found myself was far from unique. In fact it is depressingly symptomatic of the situation encompassing a vast swathe of the corporate world since the early 1990s. And I didn't have very far to look to realize that compared to some, I was doing it easy. What about my colleagues who somehow had to find "quality time" with children in their precious few extramural hours? Or the consultant who commuted in to work from Swindon—losing three hours every day in the process?

Later I came to realize just how lucky I was to have experienced these feelings, how privileged! Material affluence coupled with grinding dissatisfaction—what a wonderful foundation on which to build a more meaningful life! How many millions of people in developing countries never get the chance to discover that money can't buy happiness? Though I might never have felt so fortunate had I not been given a psychosomatic nudge in the right direction. Nothing as spectacular as a life-changing heart attack or a close brush with a dread disease. The first warning came in the form of a small red itch on my left wrist.

I can't remember exactly when it appeared, though I do

remember my bewilderment at being bitten several times again a few days later—this time on my ankle. Having spent my formative years in Africa, my instinctive reaction when I studied the raised white blotches in the midst of the inflamed pink skin was that I was looking at an ant bite. Quite how an ant had survived our Trafalgar Square offices amazed me—as I applied antiseptic skin cream I was almost in awe of it, too impressed by its survival skills to be truly irritated.

When the blotches struck again, this time on wrists and ankles simultaneously, and at home, I was forced to abandon the ant theory. Something peculiar was going on with my body. I appeared to be suffering from a strange new allergy. The prospect of breaking out in blisters immediately before an important presentation really didn't bear thinking of. I went to see my doctor immediately.

Treating the symptoms

Allergic reactions, the lugubrious Dr. Jazrat assured me, were increasingly common on our polluted planet, and could flare up or disappear at different life stages for no apparent reason. My audience with him as customarily brisk as my wait was interminably long, in a matter of minutes I was armed with a prescription for an antihistamine, and under medical instructions to pop a pill at the first sign of trouble.

The antihistamine worked wonders. Which was just as well, because the rash was soon returning in ever-more aggressive attacks. Within a matter of weeks I had become an antihistamine junkie. Using the pills as much for prevention as for cure, I recognized this wasn't a sustainable situation. Was I to get around for the next forty years with a tube of pills in my pocket?

Another consultation, this time at a clinic for complementary medicine, provided a rather different insight.

"Your body is full of toxins," Mrs. Gruber, a matronly figure in a starched white coat admonished me, after an examination. "How much coffee do you drink every day?"

This was not a subject to which I'd ever given a moment's thought. But now as I did, the cause of the red welts seemed so very obvious. "About eight cups," I admitted. The percolator was constantly, enticingly on the hot plate just outside my office.

"You're to cut it out completely," she wagged a stern index finger. "No coffee, tea, sugar, wheat, alcohol. No processed foods. Fresh food only, fruit, vegetables. Lots of water, and I'll give you something to help your liver."

There was silence while she wrote out a prescription for a liver tonic. But before handing it over, she met my eye with a concerned expression. "'Your system is highly stressed. In complementary medicine we see mind and body as part of the same continuum. You have a stressful job—" she barely waited for confirmation, "which is why you must learn to cultivate more calm, more tranquility."

Briskly handing over prescription and a separate sheet of paper, she said, "I recommend meditation. You'll find the names of some meditation classes on that list."

My emotions as I emerged from the encounter ranged from ruefulness to indignation. But it was the order to cultivate calm that took me aback more than anything. The way she'd handed over the list of meditation centers made it seem like a skill you might acquire with the same matter-of-factness as learning how to drive a car, or use Microsoft Word—as it proved to be. Only up until then, even though I was so stressed out I was quite literally breaking out in rashes, it had never occurred to me that meditation might be helpful.

The list of classes came to almost a full page, but as I ran my eye down the sheet, one entry immediately caught my attention—and not only because it would be a convenient stopping-off point on my way home. The Glebe Street Gompa in Kensington offered meditation as part of an introductory course, every Tuesday night for six weeks. As soon as I saw the words "Tibetan Buddhism" my interest was hooked. A friend of mine, Marcy Jensen, had followed Buddhism for many years. When we met, I'd often quiz her on the subject, and never failed to come away with an intriguing new perspective. Marcy would almost certainly approve of the Glebe Street Gompa, I told myself. Apart from a couple of hours of my time, what did I have to lose?

The Buddha's First Teaching

Imagine if you told a family living in abject poverty there was a treasure of gold under the dirt floor of their shanty. They would only need to remove the layers of dirt hiding it and they would be rich forever.
In the same way, we are not aware of the treasure of Buddha nature, hidden by our own ignorance and delusion.

SUBLIME CONTINUUM OF THE GREAT VEHICLE

At street level, Glebe Street Gompa looked like any other terraced Georgian house in the salubrious neighborhood just west of the South Kensington Underground station. Three steps up from pavement level led to a covered portico and a red front door, left open for visitors.

Making the decision to come here had been easy enough,

but now that I was actually on the point of no return I began to have reservations. I didn't know anything about the Glebe Street Gompa. What if the evening turned out to be a waste of time? What if it was run by a gang of tree-huggers spouting New Age clap-trap? What if they were into weird and embarrassing rituals?

Once inside, I found things reassuringly normal. A checkered-tile hallway led through to a large forest-green room lined with bookshelves from floor to ceiling. With its subdued lighting, bay windows, and comfortable armchairs, it might have been the library of a gentlemen's club in St James, were it not for the fact that everyone there was shoeless—a notice in the hallway asked visitors to remove their footwear and place it in the wooden racks provided. A few other introductory class visitors were already there in socks and stockings, browsing through the bookshelves or talking in subdued voices. Within moments of arriving, we were approached by Tom, a genial City-type who described himself as "one of the regulars." It was he who ushered the first-timers down a short flight of steps and along a wood-paneled corridor to the gompa itself.

"Gompa" is a Tibetan word meaning "place of meditation," and this was the first time I'd been in one. A large rectangular room with a gilded Buddha on an altar at the front, it was lit entirely by candles which illuminated the intricate designs and rich silks of the antique thangkas on the walls. Apart from a teaching throne to the left of the altar, the room was devoid of furniture, with only maroon-colored meditation cushions set out on the carpet in orderly rows.

I paused inside the doorway to take it all in, aware of two powerful sensations. The first was a profound sense of peace—

but was that because I subconsciously expected to feel a timeless tranquility? Or was it communicated by the serene expression on the gilded face of the Buddha and the ribbons of Nag Champa incense that wafted through the room?

The other sensation was less easy to account for, but I have subsequently learned that I am far from alone in having experienced it. Surrounded by the symbols and imagery of Tibetan Buddhism for the first time, instead of a sense of foreignness, or even aversion, what I felt was a deep-down sense of recognition, of things being the way they should be. It was like coming home.

I took my place on a cushion in the back row. I didn't want to draw attention to myself, I just wanted to sit and absorb. Looking at the magnificent arrangements of flowers on either side of the Buddha, the two rows of offering bowls set out in front of the image, I felt I was starting to de-stress just by being here. The usual chatter that filled my mind had vanished in the candlelight.

My moment of quiet reflection in this curiously engaging place was shortly disrupted by peals of laughter. It seemed that someone had arrived to the introductory class in the highest of spirits. The source of the merriment became apparent when, shortly after the class was due to begin, there was a bustle of activity and from the back of the room, in saffron and maroon robes, hurried the jovial form of Geshe Tenzing Trungpa, spiritual head of the Glebe Street Gompa.

He prostrated three times in front of the Buddha before taking his place on the teaching throne—a dais raised about a foot off the floor—and beamed at us as though still enjoying a private joke.

"Introduction Class 101," he said, his expression positively mischievous. "You all want to learn about Buddhism and how to meditate. This is very good," he nodded. "An excellent step! And you know I can show you how to meditate, not in six weeks, but in one! And not even in ninety minutes, but thirty! Knowing what to do is very, very easy. But actually accomplishing it is very, very hard."

Some important questions

He was making a serious point, but there was a lightness about him that communicated itself too. A sense of ease, almost of playfulness, that I hadn't expected. Wasn't Geshe Trungpa, referred to as Rinpoche at the center, supposed to be a very high-ranking lama? (Rinpoche, pronounced *rin-posh-eh*, literally translates as "precious".)

"It will take much longer than six weeks, or even six years to be a fully realized yogi or yogini," he continued. "Why so long? Why so difficult?" He regarded us carefully. "Because we are out of control of our minds. We have very poor concentration. You don't have to believe me—you check up for yourself. In Buddhism we like people to ask questions, we don't like blind faith. Buddha himself once said, 'Anyone who believes what I say is a fool—unless he has tried it for himself.' So you look into it." He paused, adopting a challenging expression.

"Try to focus, single-pointedly, on just one thing and tell me how long you can keep it up. Before even one minute has passed you will be thinking about tonight's dinner, and what's happening at work, and all the things you need to do at home— everything except what you decided to concentrate on."

Around the gompa heads were nodding in recognition.

"Some people call this 'the mad monkey of the mind.' Totally crazy. Jumping this way and that." He gestured in great arcs of flowing maroon. "One of the main purposes of meditation is to tame the mad monkey, to allow the mind to settle down and rest instead of all this manic activity.

"But before we come to how to meditate, we need to ask a different question. Why should we even try?" Once again he paused, looking from student to student with an expression of engaging inquiry. "Perhaps some of you are here for stress management, or to help find peace and happiness—these are good reasons." He nodded sagely. "Maybe some people want to learn to go astral traveling with the lamas?" Now his eyes were sparkling. "Much easier to fly British Airways!

"Whatever the immediate reason you have come here tonight, there is another, very important reason you should learn to meditate, and I want you to help me demonstrate what it is. Right here and now. Please will you make yourselves comfortable on your meditation cushions. Stretch your arms and legs if you like, before sitting with a nice straight back."

There was general movement as arms and legs were flexed, knuckles clicked, and shoulders rolled.

"Is everyone comfortable?" he inquired after a moment, to murmurs of assent, that same impish smile playing about his features. "Anyone not comfortable?" He scanned the mute faces.

"Very good! Now I want you to do nothing except turn your mind to your breath. Focus on the sensation as it comes in your nostrils, and then as it goes. That's all you need to do. Observe the breath entering and leaving, like a sentry at the gate."

It was the first time I'd ever been in a room with thirty people sitting in total silence, supposedly thinking about nothing except their breathing. For my own part I felt very self-conscious. Rinpoche hadn't said anything about our eyes—were they supposed to be open or closed? And how long was this going to go on for? I hoped not the whole of the next one and a half hours! I tried to focus on my breathing, but I didn't seem to be in the right frame of mind. It was the newness of this place and all the other people, I told myself. I'd probably do better in more familiar surroundings. And when I wasn't wearing my formal suit trousers.

I was thinking about the tightness of my belt when Rinpoche said, "I'm sorry, my dear, why did you move your foot?"

The class was thrown into momentary confusion. Were we still supposed to be focusing on our breathing? Rinpoche seemed to be addressing a man in the second row. (It wasn't long before we discovered that Rinpoche referred to everyone as "my dear," irrespective of gender.)

"My ankle's getting sore," came the eventual embarrassed reply. "I'm not used to sitting."

"Of course!" smiled Rinpoche. "But when I asked you to make yourself comfortable, were you not comfortable?"

Heads were now turning in the direction of the unfortunate foot-mover.

"Yes."

"Everything was okay?"

"Yes," the other faltered. "But it didn't last. I had to change my position."

"Hah!" Rinpoche clapped his hands. "You see!"

There was laughter around the room at Rinpoche's evident delight. "Thank you for being class leader in demonstrating the First Noble Truth, which is that the nature of reality, as you usually experience it—what we call *samsara*—is dissatisfaction. Even when you make yourself comfortable, it doesn't last long and you have to change your position. This applies to everything. Work. Relationships. Home. Your car. Everything!"

The Four Noble Truths

This is the true suffering.
This is true source.
This is true cessation.
This is true path.

Know the suffering.
Abandon the source.
Attain the cessation.
Meditate on the path.

THE FOUR NOBLE TRUTHS, WHEEL OF DHARMA SUTRA

Rinpoche told us that after Buddha became enlightened, his very first teachings at the Deer Park in Sarnath were the Four Noble Truths. These are often referred to as the "essence of Buddhism" because they encapsulate core teachings common to all Buddhist schools. And they are particularly relevant to Westerners today because they take precisely the same clinical approach to the human condition that we'd expect from a competent doctor if we went to him with an illness. First, Buddha diagnosed the problems we all suffer because we are human. Second, he identified the causes of them. Third, he held out the promise of a complete cure, and fourth, he gave us a prescription.

The First Noble Truth states that the underlying state of our minds is dissatisfaction. The reaction of many people hearing this for the first time is that it seems an unduly bleak diagnosis.

Sure, we all have our problems, but there is also much in our experience of life that is joyful and positive.

But Buddha wasn't saying that we spend all our lives in a state of total despair, only that the happiness or pleasure we do enjoy is of a passing nature. We may be sitting comfortably right now but the passage of time will inevitably change things. Quite apart from the challenges of everyday life, we will all, for example, experience sickness, aging, and death. Not an uplifting thought, maybe, but the accurate if uncomfortable reality.

Why is dissatisfaction so inescapable? The Second Noble Truth describes the causes of dissatisfaction. On the surface of things there are limitless reasons to account for whatever unhappiness we may experience, from momentary irritation to the most profound sorrow. But whatever the apparent cause, Buddha defined three underlying reasons which account for all dissatisfaction. These are attachment, aversion, and ignorance, sometimes referred to as desire, anger, and a misguided view of reality.

Attachment

When Buddha spoke of attachment, he wasn't saying that it's wrong to have loving feelings towards family and friends— a common misinterpretation. Some newcomers to Buddhism have the mistaken idea that they're supposed to become "detached"—distant and cut off from the world around them so that they can develop in splendid isolation. In fact, nothing could be further from Buddha's teachings, and you only need to look at the example set by the Dalai Lama to see that love and compassion, not detachment and distance, are the authentic Buddhist path.

Buddha's teachings on attachment refer specifically to our

tendency to grasp at a particular thing, person, or situation, believing that this "thing" can make us happy—a belief system that is fundamentally flawed. When we find a thing attractive, we have a natural tendency to exaggerate its positive aspects and downplay any negatives. We are encouraged along this dangerous route by the ever-eager marketing and advertising industries, whose job it is to promote products in such a way that our feelings of desire are heightened to the point that only possession of that product will bring satisfaction.

As an example, chances are that at some point you became the proud owner of a new watch. Perhaps it was a birthday gift, or maybe you bought it duty free while on holiday. Do you remember how delighted you were when you first strapped it to your wrist? Can you remember what the watch you owned before it even looked like? If you're anything like me, you would have unnecessarily checked the time on dozens of occasions those first few days, scrutinizing your watch with the thrill of new ownership. You were delighted if others around you complimented you on your elegant new accessory.

We all know what happens next, because it is the story of our lives: we get used to it. We adjust. The new watch becomes familiar. At some point the face gets scratched and it's no longer new. Perhaps the strap becomes worn. And yes, we might still think it's a good watch but when we look at it we do so without any of the pleasure we felt that first time we wore it. The watch itself hasn't changed in any significant way. So where did the wonderfulness of the watch come from, and where did it go?

Material objects, whether trivial—such as watches—or grand—such as major corporate transactions—are only one focus of attachment. Many of us have made ourselves very unhappy obsessing over potential, current, or former partners whose love, we believed at the time, would make our happiness complete. Ditto career ambitions. What percentage of the workforce truly believes that their appointment to a particular job, complete with status, remuneration package, and executive toys, will be a cause of great satisfaction? And what percentage of people occupying those sought-after jobs are greatly satisfied? As it is with the once-new watch, it is only a matter of time before our perspective changes.

Aversion

Aversion works according to the same principles, except this time it's the negatives that are exaggerated. One daily example of aversion is road rage. How is it that we, otherwise calm, balanced individuals, can be turned into impatient hotheads, swearing and delivering obscene gestures, when other drivers cause us minor inconvenience—precisely the same inconveniences to which we sometimes subject them?

All of a sudden, that other, unknown person who caused us to slam on the brakes is a reckless idiot, a selfish bastard, who should be fined or banned from driving.

It is interesting that when we experience these feelings we always think we are fully justified in our anger. It was caused by the other person, wasn't it? Isn't anger in that situation both natural and, in a way, inevitable?

The curious thing is that a different driver, who also has to brake for the same reason, may not even register that this could be a cause of irritation. This other driver may take the view that what has just happened is merely part of the give-and-take of life on the road, and keep humming along to the car radio.

Significantly, our own reaction to the incident might have

been different had we been, for example, on our way to a hot date. In different emotional circumstances our reactions to the same event vary.

So is road rage "justified," "natural," and "inevitable?"

The strange thing is that within minutes of arriving safely at our destination, we have usually completely forgotten the anger-causing incident. Which begs the question: where did the hatefulness of the other driver really come from, and where did it go?

Even more depressing than being subject to these fleeting rages are those people who cling to their negative feelings, carrying around a constant burden of slights or other miseries, unwittingly casting themselves in a victim role they feel powerless to change.

These examples of attachment and aversion are symptomatic of our ongoing engagement with the world outside us. You don't have to be a Buddhist to recognize that watches, however fancy, are not a source of enduring happiness. If it was that easy, most of us would already be living in bliss. What seemed so wonderful about our new watch, just as what now seems so ordinary about it, has only ever existed in our minds. Similarly, you don't have to be a great sage to see that the real cause of anger also exists in the mind. Most of us have encountered people who fly off the handle at the least provocation, and others who have the patience of saints, showing that what happens around us is actually a lot less important than our own response.

But strangely, even though we should know better we keep on behaving as though the real causes of happiness and anger exist "out there." We can take any day as an illustration. We might wake up in the morning and our first conscious thought is that it's Sunday. Whoopee! We roll over with pleasure and doze for a while. Getting up, we remember an obligatory lunch-time engagement we could really do without. That puts us on a downer. Then the phone rings—it's a colleague. There's been a flood in the office admin. department and they need help from anyone who can get in. Usually such a call would be a cause of grave displeasure. But today we realize we have the perfect excuse to avoid that unwanted lunch.

And so the story continues. Up. Down. Happy. Disgruntled. Like the shiny metal ball bearings in a pinball machine, it's as though we're constantly being flicked off in one direction or another by Happiness and Unhappiness switches, and we're helpless to do anything except react.

Ignorance

Which brings us to the third general cause of dissatisfaction— ignorance or wrong view. Here Buddha was referring to a specific kind of ignorance, our false belief that things and people have intrinsic characteristics all of their own. As we've already seen, this form of ignorance is inherent in both attachment and aversion.

Perhaps the easiest illustration of this form of ignorance is music. Think of your favorite music as a teenager. Now think of your parents' reaction to it. If your family was anything like mine, there was, as they say in diplomatic circles, "a difference of opinion." From time to time, to extend the metaphor, your taste in music may even have provoked "a free and frank exchange of views!"

Surprisingly, a question that's not often asked about this age-old problem is the simple one of why? Why is it that a sound so thrilling and liberating to one generation provokes such an utterly different reaction in another? They are the same sound waves, after all, striking physiologically identical receptors. So why is one person's ecstasy another's agony?

Obviously the music itself has no intrinsic attributes, or we'd all be in total agreement. It is the way we interpret the music which gives it particular qualities. Beauty truly is in the eye, or in this case the ear, of the beholder.

This may seem a subtle point, but it is one with implications which are revolutionary to our usual assumptions—because the lack of intrinsic qualities goes far beyond what's hot and what's not in chart music. It extends to every single phenomenon in the world around us. Even to bricks and mortar.

In his book *The Diamond Cutter*, Geshe Michael Roach, the charismatic Buddhist monk who helped establish a $100 million diamond business in New York City, uses the example of an office building to demonstrate how even an apparently substantial piece of Manhattan real estate has no characteristics of its own. When his company, Andin International, was running out of office space, it considered buying a building outside the Diamond District. Whether or not this was a good or bad decision depended entirely on one's point of view. Already some more commercially minded readers will have formed an opinion about the wisdom of this move from the one sentence I've written about it. Buying a building instead of paying rent— good. Moving outside the established industry area—bad. But what if reduced costs outside the Diamond District gave the company the ability to offer better deals in the marketplace? Good. Or if property values in that part of Manhattan were hit? Bad.

Looking at it from an employee point of view, those who traveled in from New Jersey thought it was a good move—

they'd have a shorter commute to work. For exactly the opposite reason, employees from Brooklyn were unhappy about it. And so it went on. The directors and staff of Andin could all visit their proposed new office building, look at it, walk around it, metaphorically kick its tires, but whether or not it would make for a better workplace depended entirely on individual points of view.

And so it is with everything. The overweight housewife in Swansea is the voluptuous beauty in Swaziland. The entrepreneur encouraged to take pride in his achievements in Los Angeles is shunned as a *nouveau riche* upstart in London. For much of the time we act on the basis of assumptions—often unspoken—about what would be a "good" thing or a "bad" thing without recognizing that there is no such thing as objective reality. The way the world looks, sounds, tastes, and feels is different to each one of us because of the way we interpret it. For this reason, Buddhists use the phrase "dependent arising" to describe all phenomena. The way that things exist, or arise in our minds, depends, among other things, on how we perceive them.

This is a very important subject, and one to which we'll return later. But on that first visit I made to the Glebe Street Gompa, the notion that everything and everyone around me might be a '"dependent arising" was both obvious, and at the same time a novel idea with profound implications.

The superstition of materialism

"The Second Noble Truth," Rinpoche looked around the class, "tells us that the causes for our dissatisfaction come from attachment, aversion, and our false belief that certain things outside us have the ability to make us happy or unhappy from their own side. But check up on this for yourself. The happiness or unhappiness isn't coming from out there. It's coming from in here," and he touched his heart.

"The most popular way to achieve happiness in the West is by rearranging what's out there. Our homes, our cars, our girlfriends and boyfriends. But you can see why this plan is doomed to failure. Those things out there we spend so much time trying to get right don't have any qualities from their own side. The nice things about them are really projections of our minds. And because our minds are so agitated, changing from one moment to the next, those nice qualities quickly change too."

That mischievous smile reappeared as he rocked back on his meditation cushion. "I like to ask my students, 'Are you superstitious?'" His eyes twinkled. "They usually say, 'Oh no, Rinpoche! I walk under ladders. I like black cats. If the mirror in the bathroom cracks, it doesn't worry me!'" His chuckle was infectious. "But what is superstition? It is the false association between certain causes—like mirrors breaking—and the supposed effects. Which is why I say Westerners are the most superstitious people on the planet! They believe in associations that don't exist. Associations between what's out there and what's in here.

"Of course we don't have to remain deluded. The Third Noble Truth tells us that it is possible to reduce dissatisfaction, more and more, until we remove it completely. The Fourth Noble Truth tells us how to set about doing this.

"It's a big subject and I will be teaching it for the next few weeks. But you can see already that our main area of work will be the mind, because this is the source of all our happiness and unhappiness. It is where our idea of reality is created. Buddhism teaches us how to rearrange not what's out there, but what's in here."

As he looked about the room, for a moment we all seemed to be sharing in Rinpoche's playfulness and wisdom.

"Buddha was once asked to describe the essence of his teachings," Rinpoche said. "Do you know what he replied? 'Abandon harmfulness. Cultivate goodness. Subdue your mind.'"

"You will already have a good idea about what is meant by abandoning harmfulness and cultivating goodness. These are universal truths shared by all of the great traditions. But when Buddha spoke of subduing the mind, he was talking about meditation.

"On the surface of things," Rinpoche continued, "subduing the mind sounds like a nice thing to do. Which one of us doesn't want to have more tranquility, less agitation? But understanding the Four Noble Truths, you can see why meditation is about much more than staying calm in traffic jams. Practiced properly, over a period of time, meditation changes our whole interpretation of reality. It helps us break free from the superstition that we need certain things and people to make us happy. It allows us to find our own true nature."

In the silence of the gompa, we had already caught a glimpse of our hitherto unsuspected superstition.

"If you allow a glass of murky storm water to stand, eventually the dirt settles and you are left with only clear water. It's the same with meditation." Rinpoche paused, his smile beatific. "Eventually we discover that the true nature of our mind is nothing except pure clarity, awareness—and bliss."

3. How to Meditate

We are what we repeatedly do.

ARISTOTLE

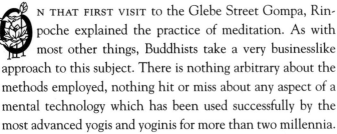N THAT FIRST VISIT to the Glebe Street Gompa, Rinpoche explained the practice of meditation. As with most other things, Buddhists take a very businesslike approach to this subject. There is nothing arbitrary about the methods employed, nothing hit or miss about any aspect of a mental technology which has been used successfully by the most advanced yogis and yoginis for more than two millennia.

If, while reading this chapter, you are struck by the simplicity of some of the practices outlined, it is as well to remember Rinpoche's observation that understanding what to do is not the hard part. The hard part is putting it into practice. In the words of the Dalai Lama, "When we speak of the city of enlightenment it sounds very near and very easy to attain; but when it comes to practice, suddenly it seems very difficult to attain, very far in the distance. This is the contradiction between our thoughts and our application."

Meditation practice and benefits

Just as buying the most sophisticated in-home gym equipment is no guarantee of a body beautiful, so too knowing the wisdom of the most advanced lamas is of little purpose unless it's actually used.

The Tibetans have a word to describe the best approach to meditation. That word translates approximately as "joyous perseverance," an approach any gym junkie would endorse and which also serves as a useful reminder when we find ourselves contemplating the "stay in bed" approach to mind training!

Why does it take so much effort to achieve something as simple as mental clarity and awareness? Quite simply, it's because it goes against all previous conditioning. We've lived with a ceaseless tide of internal chatter for so long that it's only when we take the unusual step of focusing the spotlight of our attention on the mind itself, observing its antics at close quarters and in real time, that we discover we have a lunatic in the attic.

Trying to tame the mad monkey mind is, in many ways, like a flabby middle-aged businessman trying to recover his youthful profile on the step machine. It hurts because we're just not used to it. We are confronted by the consequences of decades of bad habits and ill-discipline. We are forced to use mental muscles we didn't even know existed. Wouldn't it be easier just to give up, and instead enjoy a nice big internal talkfest, garnished with disjointed reflections and lashings of fantasy?

Actually, it wouldn't—not in the long run. Because just as fit and healthy retirees enjoy a far superior quality of life to their overweight and unhealthy counterparts, so too the quality of life of those who have cultivated a strong level of peace and equanimity can't be compared to that of their more troubled, vulnerable peers.

So what are some of the practical nuts and bolts of meditation?

The seven-point meditation posture

To begin with, it's important to get into the best posture to concentrate. As mind and body are interdependent, in a certain pose the mind naturally becomes calmer, more stable. This wisdom is shared by many of the great traditions and is encapsulated in the following seven points:

- Sit cross-legged. Don't attempt a lotus position, or even half lotus, unless you're very comfortable with it. A regular cross-legged posture, supported by a cushion to help raise the spine, is just fine. If you can't manage sitting on the floor, it's acceptable to use a chair.
- Rest your hands in your lap, right hand in the left, like a pair of shells, thumb tips meeting. Ideally your thumb tips should be at the level of your navel.
- Keep a straight back. This is an essential instruction, given the importance of the back to the central nervous system. In Buddhism there is a further understanding of the subtle energies which pervade our bodies and which also support consciousness when our backs are straight.
- Mouth, jaw, and tongue should be relaxed—not slack, not tight. By placing the tip of the tongue behind your front teeth, you can help control the build-up of saliva.
- Tilt the head slightly forward. Not too far or you may fall asleep!

- Eyes should be either half-closed, gazing unfocused onto the floor in front or, if it's easier, closed, but not too tightly.
- Shoulders should be level and arms jutting out comfortably, allowing air to circulate around the body.

Objective setting

Now that you're buckled onto your meditation cushion, what next? Just as any successful meeting or new enterprise is best started with clear objectives in mind, so too Buddhists begin each meditation session by reminding themselves exactly what it is they're trying to achieve.

For a beginner, a good objective could be as follows:

> By the practice of this meditation
> I will become more calm and relaxed,
> More efficient and happier in all that I do,
> Both for my own sake and for others.

How will we achieve this objective? Through a process which enables us to experience the expansive spaciousness which naturally arises when we calm our minds.

The object of meditation

Correctly seated, and motivated, the next thing needed is an object of meditation. You can choose from a variety, including mantras, visualizations, and external objects. But perhaps the most widely used foundation practice object is the breath.

As a meditation object, the breath has a number of powerful advantages. It can always be accessed—unlike, for example, a complicated mantra which might escape you in a moment of high stress, or a physical object which you might not have with you when it's most needed. What's more, the simple act of focusing on the breath has a marked systemic effect. Usually when we pay attention to our breathing it quite naturally begins to slow, triggering a chain of physiological events which result in our becoming calmer, more relaxed. In a later section we look at some of the psychological and physiological benefits of meditation in more detail. But for now, here are two alternative meditation practices, using the breath as the object. In both cases, the aim is to focus our minds on the object of meditation with single-pointed concentration.

Meditation technique number 1:
Breath counting
The idea here is to mentally count each breath on exhalation, typically for ten breaths, before repeating the exercise.

Place the focus of your attention at the tip of your nostrils, like a sentry, and observe the flow of air as you breathe in, and then out. As you breathe out, count the number "one" in your mind, then on the next out-breath "two," then "three," "four," and so on. Don't focus on anything else—for example, don't follow the air traveling into your lungs, or your ribcage rising and falling. Don't allow your mind to wander from the tip of your nostrils. Don't fall asleep.

Sound easy? Try it!

Very quickly you'll find all manner of thoughts arriving, uninvited, in your mind. There's every chance you'll be so distracted by them you can't even count to ten! This is called gross agitation and it happens to us all. When it does, once you realize you've lost the object of meditation, simply refocus on the breath and start back at one again. Don't beat yourself up about your lapse of attention. Don't fool yourself into thinking you're a special case that isn't going to respond to this weirdo meditation business so you might as well give up right now. Our minds are wondrously inventive at coming up with reasons to avoid discipline: don't fall for any of them!

If you experience a lot of gross agitation in the beginning, don't try making it to ten, but see if you can reach four, then, when you feel comfortable with that, build up to a regular count of seven. When I started meditating, for many months my main practice was simply to spend ten minutes each day counting to four. A simple practice, perhaps, but one which was to have far-reaching effects.

Once concentration improves, your focus on the breath will become sharper. Now you can note the start of each in-breath, how it builds up, then how it tails off. The gap between in-breath and out-breath. Then the start, middle, and fading away of each exhalation. The gap at the end of each exhalation. As you get further into a meditation session, your breathing will probably slow, and you'll become more and more conscious of the gap between out-breath and in-breath. What do you focus on then? Only the absence of breath. This may not seem an ambitious goal but, rest assured, it is not only profoundly calming, it also leads directly to the very heart of Buddhist wisdom.

Meditation technique number 2:
Nine-cycle breath meditation
Another breath-focused technique goes like this: focus on inhaling through your left nostril and exhaling through your right for three breaths. Then inhaling through your right nostril and exhaling through your left for three breaths. Then inhaling and exhaling through both nostrils for three breaths.

Because it's a slightly busier meditation than the first one, you may find it easier to accomplish. Just as in the case of breath counting, however, having firmly placed your concentration on the breath you should aim both to maintain that concentration and develop it, observing the nature of each in-breath and out-breath, and the spaces in between, as described before.

The point here is not, physically, to breathe only through right and left nostrils, but to practice focusing one's attention on the process.

Mindfulness and awareness

This is the way you slip through into your innermost home:
Close your eyes, and surrender.

Rumi, Sufi poet

Early on in your meditation practice you will discover the two main obstacles to meditation—agitation and dullness. Gross agitation causes you to completely lose the object of meditation, so that you have to bring the mind back, like a disobedient child, gently but firmly. With subtle agitation you are still able to maintain the object of meditation, but experience a variety of distractions, from the constant threat of total disruption to less intrusive disturbances.

When we experience dullness, on the other hand, our concentration is threatened by sleepiness. Instead of focusing on the object of meditation, we find ourselves nodding off.

In countering these two main hindrances, we have two main tools at our disposal. *Mindfulness* means keeping the object of our meditation in mind, and not allowing our concentration to stray. *Awareness* means being watchful of what our mind is actually doing—"like a spy."

My initial reaction on hearing this teaching was that Rinpoche was merely splitting hairs. Concentration, mindfulness, awareness—it's all the same thing, surely? At first glance it may seem that way, but once you begin to experience meditation practice, you realize that there *are* differences and that being able to make seemingly subtle but important distinctions can be a real aid to progress. By simply being conscious of mindfulness and awareness as a starting point, then incorporating them in practice, little by little we are able to increase our effectiveness as meditators.

Ending a meditation

Just as it's a good idea to begin each meditation with a clear statement of objectives, at the end it's useful to reinforce this statement, thereby helping condition our minds for future sessions. A useful dedication might be as follows:

By the practice of this meditation
I am becoming increasingly calm and relaxed,
More efficient and happier in all that I do,
Both for my own sake and for others.

Getting the most out of meditation

The mechanics of a meditation session are fairly easy to understand. But how do we make sure that meditation has a positive effect on our lives?

Make meditation part of your daily routine

Our bodies are creatures of habit. Each of us has our own daily biorhythms and the idea is to work with those rhythms, not overlook them. Finding a good time of the day to meditate, and sticking with that time, is very important.

Most long-term meditators I know start the day with meditation. That way at least, you're only likely to be up against agitation as opposed to both agitation and dullness! Getting up, showering, then shutting myself away for a while is my own routine, and that of many other busy Buddhists I know.

Perhaps you have to start work early, or have children who need to be supervised. Even setting the alarm clock just fifteen minutes earlier will, if you keep it up, prove life changing. It almost goes without saying that it's best to practice in a place where your privacy will be respected, and you will be interruption free.

An analogy I like goes like this: if you want to start a fire by rubbing two sticks together, it's not going to work if you rub for a while and give up—leaving the sticks to go cold—before making another fruitless attempt. Consistency is required. In the same way, if you really want to achieve results from meditation, it's important to make it part of your daily routine, as opposed to an ad hoc, "when I can find the time" activity. Ten minutes every day is better than two hours on the weekend.

What happens if you are interrupted by something beyond your control? Simply calm your mind, repeat your objective, and start at the beginning again.

And if you miss a session? Don't worry about it—you don't have to do "extra time" the next day, unless you feel like it. The important point is to make meditation a normal and enjoyable part of your everyday life.

Manage your expectations

"A common mistake in practice," says the Dalai Lama, "is to have expectations of quick results . . . I feel it is more wise to practice without eyes anxious for signs of quick enlightenment."

Just as we find it easy to accept that it would take years of intense workouts to build the body of a Stallone or a Schwarzenegger, so too we need to accept that building the mind of a Dalai Lama isn't just going to happen after a few months of mental pushups. Most of us, however, would be content to forgo Arnie's rippling biceps or Sylvester's washboard stomach and settle for a more robust and healthy version of ourselves. So too with meditation. While our ultimate aim may be enlightenment, our short-term goals need to be more realistic—such as experiencing less agitation and more genuine contentment.

And the timeframe? This depends on how much you put into it. Genuine transformation of the mind is an evolutionary process, not a revolutionary one. Long-ingrained, negative mental habits take time to conquer. If you persist, however, you will inevitably progress, in the same way that doing aerobics every day can only improve your cardiovascular system. Of course you may not always feel you're getting anywhere. A wonderfully low-distraction meditation session may very well be followed by one in which your mind acts not only like a mad monkey, but like one which has just raided the drug store! Don't let this bother you. Let go of expectations. Meditation is like a stock market portfolio— in the short term it may very well go down as well as up.

But over a period of months, then years, change becomes

more profound. Gross agitation fades to the point you may even forget you ever had trouble with it. In the words of the Buddhist master Shantideva:

> There is nothing whatsoever
> That is not made easier through acquaintance.

Enlightenment isn't an event which can be observed, like graduating from university. It is, rather, a process—the most meaningful journey of transformation we can choose to make.

Integrate your practice

The Buddhist definition of meditation is an interesting one: acquainting the mind with virtue. One significant implication here is that meditation isn't just something that begins and ends on the meditation cushion. Mindfulness and awareness should be integrated into everyday activities so that ultimately our whole life is a meditation.

The use of awareness quickly reveals that much of our daily activity is alarmingly mindless. We may sit down to our favorite meal in front of the TV and perhaps we'll notice, and relish, the first couple of mouthfuls, but within moments our attention is distracted by what's on the news. For the rest of the meal we're not paying any attention to our food. Eating has become a mechanical exercise. Our minds are elsewhere. More worrying—we don't even need to be watching TV for this to happen!

The same can be said of a large proportion of our other activities. Walking to work on a beautiful morning, instead of enjoying the warmth of the sun on our faces we might find ourselves tensing up in anticipation of a difficult meeting. That widespread condition, "Sundayitis," arises when instead of enjoying our weekend recreation, our concentration on the prospect of another working week makes us so wound-up or depressed that we rob ourselves of the limited leisure hours that we have.

Very frequently we might be physically present but not really experiencing what's going on around us. The lights are on, to use that old cliché, but there's no one at home. We're not mentally present and living in each moment.

I like the story of the novice monk who asked a very much older yogi, "What do you do, as an enlightened being?"

To which the other replied, after a pause, "I walk and I eat and I sleep."

The young monk was taken aback. "But I also walk and eat and sleep," he responded.

"Yes," the other smiled. "But when I walk, I walk. When I eat, I eat. And when I sleep, I sleep."

Some Buddhist teachers exhort their students to put sticky labels demanding "What are you thinking?" in various places in their home or office as a means of introducing the practice of mindfulness. And it's certainly useful to ambush ourselves each day and ask this question. For while no one is denying the value of analysis, reflection, planning, and other cognitive "up-time," the simple reality is that we spend a lot of our day engaged in undirected internal chatter which at best is of no value, and at worst directly increases our own anxiety and stress levels. How much better would it be to focus on the activity of the moment, and actually experience it? To savor the whole meal instead of just the first mouthful?

The benefits of meditation

Lam Rim teachings tell us that meditation is an essential part of our goal to gain more control of our own minds. With greater mindfulness and awareness we will be more successful in progressively eliminating the attachment, anger, and ignorance which cause us such unhappiness.

It is also the case, however, that meditation has some extremely positive side effects which kick in long before you might seriously consider enlightenment as a possibility. In the next section I describe how taking up basic breath-counting meditation helped me, both personally and professionally, to an extent I would never have dreamed possible. I also refer to an extraordinary case of healing known to me. And a visit to any meditation or Buddhist center will soon produce a wealth of stories about how meditation has benefited its practitioners in a variety of ways, from the prosaic to the profound.

The physical benefits of meditation are less well known, but as mind–body technology in the West catches up with the intuitive and ancient wisdom of the East, we are beginning to understand just how profoundly meditation can alter our health at a cellular level. Much of the work in this area has been done using practitioners of Transcendental Meditation, or TM, as subjects, mainly because TM is widely practiced in the USA and thus there are large, readily available populations from which to draw samples. TM involves mantra recitation, not dissimilar to some much-used Tibetan Buddhist practices.

According to UCLA physiologist R. Keith Wallace, meditators who used TM regularly for up to five years had an average biological age five years lower than their chronological age.

Those who'd been meditating for more than five years had an average biological age that was twelve years lower than their chronological age. Other studies have shown that DHEA, the only hormone known to decline directly with age, is much higher in regular meditators. In fact, people who meditate regularly have the average DHEA levels of people ten to twelve years younger, possibly explaining why so many Buddhists look somewhat younger than their age!

Groundbreaking work by Professor Richard Davidson, of the Laboratory for Affective Neuroscience at the University of Wisconsin–Madison, showed that volunteers who underwent just an eight-week course in Buddhist meditation showed greater activity in the left frontal cortex than the right. People who are depressed, stressed, or angry tend to have greater activity in the right, whereas left cortex activity is associated with happiness and relaxation. The world's media reacted with astonishment to his findings when they were released in May, 2002. Could people train themselves to be happy, they asked breathlessly?

There can be little doubt that as science catches up with practice the benefits of meditation will be even more accurately defined and documented—although the independent validation already available is powerful enough.

For most of us who practice meditation, however, the latest "breakthroughs" in scientific studies, while welcome, are very secondary. Just as we don't need experimental data to persuade us that ice cream tastes good on a hot day, neither do we need scientific methodology to convince us of the benefits of meditation. We already have our own direct, personal experience of this powerful practice which, for most of us, is the best way we know of coming home.

Seeing the world more clearly

It is your own awareness right now. It is simple, natural and clear.
Why say, "I don't understand what the mind is"?
There is nothing to think about,
Just permanent clear consciousness.

PADMASAMBHAVA

I hadn't really known what to expect on that first visit to the Glebe Street Gompa, but it turned out to be a challenging experience. Yes, I'd started to learn about meditation, but Rinpoche had also made me aware of many other issues. Up until then, if anyone else had suggested I wasn't firmly in control of my own mind, I would have reacted with blistering indignation.

But there could be no denying my less-than-enlightening experience on the meditation cushion. Nor could there be any escaping the self-evident truth of Rinpoche's explanation of how our experience of reality is far more a projection of our own minds than we care to admit. Changing the projection was, I realized, not going to happen simply because I wanted to.

And I faced a very practical problem: when was I supposed to meditate? I got up every morning around 7:00 A.M., and no sooner had I showered, dressed, and downed a bowl of cereal than I was out the door to fight for a place on the train at Clapham Junction. My working day was invariably a hectic round of issuing media releases, chasing journalists, meeting clients, and working on new business presentations. By the time it was all over, and I'd found my way home again, it was rarely earlier than seven thirty, and quite often after eight. Tired, jaded, and stressed out, my wife and I would pour ourselves a glass or two of wine, make supper or go out to a local restaurant, then slump in front of the TV for an hour or two before collapsing into bed. Next morning, the whole routine would be repeated.

I decided that getting up before seven was my only real option, difficult though it seemed. Setting my alarm for 6:50 A.M. as I got into bed one evening, I prepared to begin meditating.

I can still remember how awkward and strange I felt that first week. Self-consciousness was my greatest, most immediate cause of agitation. Without the benefit of Rinpoche's reassuring instructions and calm logic, I was also assailed by doubts. How could just thinking about my breathing change anything? What could ten minutes in the morning do to counteract twelve hours of stress every day? Was I just wasting valuable sleeping time?

Getting more used to the routine, I became aware of how noisy our flat was even first thing in the morning. Directly under the flight path to Heathrow, the low rumble of jets would sound overhead at least once a minute. There'd be the rattle of the milk van, the low drone of the street sweeper, the occasional tire screech and engine growl as an angry motorist pulled away from nearby traffic lights.

Through all this, I didn't even try counting to ten. Ten was Mount Everest as far as I was concerned. Four presented quite enough of a challenge!

I wasn't sure if I was achieving anything, even after I managed a more focused session, but I knew I had to give meditation a few weeks to work. Right from the start, though, I was aware of something different in my life. At moments during the day I'd realize, *I meditated this morning,* and that simple thought induced a momentary positive sense that for at least ten minutes that day I'd done something useful. I was still just as stressed and irritated but occasionally I would remember, *I can get back some of the calm I feel when I meditate* and, closing my eyes, I'd focus on my breathing, bringing that morning's peacefulness into the moment.

As for Mrs. Gruber's other directives, their combined effect was both instant and dramatic. For a week I cut out all coffee, alcohol, and wheat products, and made special efforts to flush out my system with water. And for the first week in many months I was troubled by not a single rash, nor even the hint of one. I still kept Dr. Jazrat's antihistamine tablets on me at all times, but soon found they'd become redundant.

I wasn't all that strict about Mrs. Gruber's orders. I kept off the booze and bread for only about two weeks, but I followed her instructions about coffee, which I didn't touch for six weeks. It was no great hardship, and in the meantime I'd read up on caffeine intolerance to understand better how it worked. After my first cup I waited for a telltale sign but there was none at all. I soon found that I could drink a couple of cups a day and be fine. And I've never had to take another antihistamine tablet.

The obvious success of my war on hives had made me realize the importance of balance, and strengthened my enthusiasm for meditation. While I didn't manage it every day, I did most mornings. Over the next few weeks, then months, it became a natural part of my life. Within six months, it was something I didn't ever want to go without.

The first, most apparent, benefit was a new and evolving sense of perspective. Rinpoche's analogy of the glass of murky storm water left to settle took on a very personal significance as the world about me was revealed with unprecedented clarity.

Having abandoned my attempts to become a published

author, and finding my every energy absorbed in public relations, I decided that I might as well advance my career as far as possible. Strategic planning was my forte, but most agencies, including the one where I worked, simply didn't have use for a full-time planner, which meant I spent most of my time on other activities.

So when I was approached by a headhunter about an opportunity with a high-powered firm which valued strategic planning and was prepared to pay handsomely for it, my most fervent ambitions appeared, quite effortlessly, about to be realized. The company profile was right. The opportunities were boundless. All in all, the offer seemed too good to be true.

As it proved to be.

Within weeks of starting the new job, I realized I'd made a terrible mistake. What I thought of as the strategic planning process, and what my new employers understood by the term, were two completely different things. What's more, the culture of the new company was the very opposite of the collegial environment I'd enjoyed until very recently. Here, consultants stayed firmly in their offices, reluctant to share ideas and closing their doors for whispered telephone conversations. Then there was the personality clash between myself and one of the directors, who seemed to have taken it upon himself to make my life as unpleasant as possible. To cap it all, a short while after I joined it, the agency was propelled into the headlines, accused of dirty tricks.

Three months into the job, I found myself doing what I'd advised countless friends and colleagues in the past never to do: I resigned without another job to go to.

I had a desperate, though not altogether crazy, plan. The public relations industry was buoyant at the time and, having spoken to several recruitment specialists, I felt sure that something would turn up soon. In the meantime, I had a couple of freelance opportunities in the offing.

Where, you may well ask, was my newfound clarity and awareness in all of this? What use were the months of meditation help when my PR career hit the wall at high speed? Well . . . what surprised me, through all the shenanigans, was just how calm I remained. It was as though I was able to watch the unraveling of my dreams and expectations with a curious serenity, even well-being.

I don't regard myself as a particularly stoical type, so my potentially disastrous career move had left me much less troubled than I would have expected to be. In some ways it was sheer relief at not having to go into that hated office again. But against this had to be balanced the need to pay the mortgage and to revive a now-troubled career. In addition, I was forced to abandon any idea that my career would be a smooth, let alone effortless, series of steps to the top.

As it happened, I soon found myself busy with freelance work. Because what I did was quite specialized, and by now I knew consultants in a number of different agencies, once I'd knocked on a few doors my phone started to ring with fresh assignments. In addition, several former colleagues began referring clients who were too small for an agency but who made solid clients for a self-employed consultant.

Much to my own surprise, within months I found I was earning more money than I ever had as an employee, while working fewer hours—*and* without the stress of the commuter hour in London. For the first time in years I felt relaxed, and I was enjoying the novelty of being my own boss and experiencing a freedom I'd never felt before.

In hindsight I genuinely don't know if my first halting steps in meditation were in some arcane way the cause of my new-found independence. But I'm certain that I weathered the storm, and discovered a different way of working, with far greater equanimity than I otherwise might have.

And there was another significant development that I knew arose directly from this fresh sense of perspective. Now with wonderful time to walk around Wandsworth and Clapham Commons in the evenings, mulling over events of the day and things in general, my thoughts strayed back to writing.

I had no intention of completing another unpublished novel. Compulsive scribbler though I may be, after ten failed attempts even I knew better than to try that again! This time I approached writing from a slightly different direction.

For a couple of years, the subject of spin doctoring had been much in the media, but the fact of the matter was that very few people had any idea how spin doctors really operated, how thoroughly enmeshed they were with the news media or, with a few notable exceptions, who these underworld creatures even were.

Having spent so much of my adult life in the PR industry, and having worked for a company recently accused of skullduggery, I felt well qualified to fill this information gap. In an illuminating moment I realized that for the first time in my life, instead of trying to create a genre or story that would appeal to publishers, instead of attempting to second-guess the passing whims and fancies of the book trade, I would be writing about what I knew best.

This time I didn't sit down to write an entire book as I had in the past, but drafted just a few sample chapters. I researched and wrote a short proposal for a book called *The Invisible Per-*

suaders. And, avoiding further disappointments with literary agents, I sent the material directly to half a dozen nonfiction editors.

My modus operandi was different, but so too was my state of mind. This time I really didn't care if the proposal was accepted or not. Of course I sought a positive response, but having invested so little in the project, if nothing much came of it, I wouldn't be too disappointed. I thought I had the right subject, and was in the right place, but was this the right time—or had publishers already commissioned a book to fill this apparently obvious gap in the market? Only time would tell.

The healing power of meditation

About ten days after sending out my proposals, the phone rang. In one of those strange coincidences in life, the voice at the other end belonged to someone who had been in my thoughts a great deal in the past few weeks. Since visiting Glebe Street Gompa I'd often wondered how she was. Marcy Jensen was on the line from Los Angeles. She was about to pass through town. Would I be free to meet up with her?

A few evenings later I went to visit Marcy, inhabiting her usual suite at The Savoy. Marcy is considerably older than I am—my wife, Janmarie, often teases me about "David's older women." We'd met some years previously through a mutual friend and immediately hit it off.

Marcy was the first person I knew who called herself a Buddhist. In the past we'd spent many hours talking about the Dharma—I'd been intrigued by her stories about reincarnated lamas and clairvoyance. But all our stimulating conversations of the past had been overshadowed just six months previously, when Marcy had phoned from California to tell me she'd been diagnosed with breast cancer.

It had been hard staying in touch with her since then. The London-Los Angeles time difference made things difficult, and Marcy didn't like emails or even faxes. The few occasions we'd spoken by phone had never been at good moments for her. The result was that I felt both out of touch and concerned. The fact that she was in London in itself seemed positive news, but having lost my mother after a long and wearying battle against cancer, I knew not to expect or hope too much. This evening I'd learn the truth—alone, because Janmarie had a work function.

It was mainly because of Marcy's involvement with Tibetan Buddhism that I'd been led to the Glebe Street Gompa. The wife of a once famous Hollywood actor, she'd lived most of her life in the hills of Bel Air, among a coterie of household-name stars and eccentric human collectibles. There was the Hollywood heartthrob who wore corsets to conceal his pot-belly. The English lord who lived on a diet of cheese and champagne. The Parisian movie director who'd trained his English sheepdog to remove champagne corks with its teeth.

A raconteur with a fund of the most outrageous stories, Marcy enjoyed an audience and was always fun to be with. Whenever she was passing through town, which happened at least twice a year, we'd get together.

It was Marcy who had first told me the facts of Shakyamuni Buddha's life. "The historical Buddha who lived two and a half thousand years ago is usually called Shakyamuni Buddha," she'd told me, "*Shakya* being his family name and *muni* translating as 'Able One.' But the name given him by his parents was Siddhartha, meaning 'Aim Attained.'"

Siddhartha's background was far from ordinary; he was born in 624 B.C. to a royal family whose kingdom occupied part of what is Nepal today. From the little we know of Prince Siddhartha's childhood, he seems to have excelled at both school and sports until at the age of sixteen he was married to a young girl who soon bore him a son.

Through his years as a child and young adult, Prince Siddhartha's father had tried to shield him from the darker side of life. This concern went beyond normal fatherly protectiveness, for around the time of the prince's birth, King Shuddhodana had been warned by a fortune-teller that his son, once confronted by evidence of suffering, would want to leave home.

Which was exactly how things turned out. Sneaking out to the gardens surrounding the city, Prince Siddhartha's encounters with old age, sickness, and death—the very things his father had tried his best to sanitize—were followed by a powerful encounter with a serene monk. Shaken by these experiences, and attracted by the apparent tranquility of the reflective life, when Prince Siddhartha asked if he too could become a monk his father not only refused, he put a detachment of soldiers on round-the-clock duty to stop him from trying to leave home.

But at the age of twenty-nine, Prince Siddhartha managed to escape, resolving to become an ascetic. For six years he became an itinerant monk, living in extreme austerity and focusing all his energies on meditation. During this time, deprived of both food and sleep, he became skeletal in appearance. When he realized that his privations were weakening him, he accepted food from a village woman and bathed in a nearby river. Strength renewed, he continued to meditate, eventually becoming a Buddha, or "Awakened One," under what is now known as the Bodhi Tree, or Tree of Awakening.

A short time after this, he made his way to the deer park of Sarnath, outside the city of Benares, where he gave his first teaching—the Four Noble Truths. He spent the next forty-five years teaching the Dharma, until his death at the age of eighty.

So much for the outline of Shakyamuni Buddha's life. But I remembered that Marcy had been at pains to emphasize that Shakyamuni is only one of many millions of Buddhas. True, he is regarded as a "world Buddha," because of the huge impact of his teachings—but there were two "world Buddhas" before him, and others are said to be coming. But what is of importance is to realize that Buddha was not a god or a special holy man, or even unique. He was, rather, a living example of what we can all achieve if we follow what is sometimes called the Middle Way—at its most basic level, a path between the extremes of hedonism and austerity. Not only are we all capable of becoming Awakened—this state is our ultimate destiny. And once we realize our own Awakened or Buddha nature, we can move in an infinite variety of ways to help others.

Arriving at Marcy's hotel suite, as the door flew open I took her in—the pageboy-cut grey hair, the mischievous hazel eyes, the hands adorned with a dozen costume rings.

"You look just the same as ever!" I told her, delighted, as we hugged.

"Just the same, but completely different!" she chimed, leading me through to her sitting room. "Shampoo?"

She waved towards the ice bucket of Taittinger, her perennial favorite.

"Thank you. I'll pour," I offered. "I'm pleased your treatment hasn't put you off it."

"Obligatory, my dear!" she said, sinking into one of her sofas.

After I'd poured two glasses and handed her one, I joined her on the sofa. "To your very good health." For once the toast had special significance.

"Oh!" She tossed her head after taking a sip, "I'm perfectly all right."

"So the treatment was—"

"Look," she tugged at her hair. "All my own. The two girls—" she thrust her sixty-something bosom at me wickedly, "intacto!"

The contrast with my mother's experience of breast cancer, or rather, the treatment of it, could hardly be greater. The toxic side effects of chemotherapy had been far worse than anything inflicted by the disease itself. After her mastectomy, the chemotherapy that followed resulted in my poor Mum losing all her hair and having to wear a wig. Nausea and sleeping problems troubled her for months and her face had taken on a chalky pallor. Watching her from the sidelines, having to endure all that, had been heartbreaking.

The power of Medicine Buddha

Marcy kicked off her mules and, tucking her legs under herself, told me how as soon as she'd been diagnosed she got in touch with her Buddhist teacher, a Tibetan lama who divided his time between Los Angeles and Canada. Over the years her confidence in his apparently clairvoyant judgment had grown to the extent that she'd accept his advice over that offered by anyone else—including the medical experts.

"I told him that doctors were advising chemotherapy." She pulled a face. "I'd asked them if surgery wouldn't be enough. I was less scared of surgery—even a mastectomy. But the specialist had told me that chemo was the recommended treatment to prevent any spread.

"Lama listened to everything I said, and I was half expecting him to tell me about some alternative treatment. Chinese herbs, something like that. But his first reaction was to go all stern on me. 'This is a good opportunity to strengthen your practice,'" she mimicked. "He was quite clear about what I should do, telling me to follow the doctors' recommendations—with just one qualifier. I must practice Medicine Buddha meditation as much as possible. He was very strong on this. I got a bit weepy and asked if everything would be all right, but he was very strict. At first I couldn't believe how unsympathetic he was being, he seemed so uncaring. Later I realized he was only doing it for my own good. He wanted me to understand this was no time to go soft. There was nothing he could do. But he gave me clear directions on what I must do for myself. He said, 'If you practice with strong commitment, you have nothing to fear.'"

Medicine Buddha meditation involves reciting a mantra in combination with certain visualizations. These include visualizing a dark blue-colored Buddha emanating a powerful healing light which enters the body, removing all illness and causes of illness. Like other tantra practices, the power of Medicine Buddha depends on the mind of the practitioner, not on an external deity. Both the words and images of Medicine Buddha practice exist as powerful tools to help unlock specific aspects of our own Buddha nature. In short, the practice is less a request to some external entity to heal us than it is a means by which we access a power we already have, which helps us heal ourselves.

Remembering her teacher's uncompromising instruction, Marcy immediately began a new routine in which she had three hour-long sessions a day practicing Medicine Buddha.

"Lama was right," she said seriously. "It *was* a good opportunity to strengthen my practice. The world suddenly looks a lot different when you feel your life is about to be taken away from you. And I don't need to tell you why I was dreading the chemo."

Marcy hadn't expected any side effects after the first lot of chemotherapy, but it was early days—she was due to go in every ten days for a two-month period. But after the second and then the third chemotherapy sessions were followed by no side effects, she spoke to her oncologist. Was she receiving the correct dosage, she wanted to know. Shouldn't she be feeling nauseous? Shrugging his shoulders, the oncologist agreed her experience was unusual, but told her that some patients had a higher tolerance for chemotherapy than others.

"Lama happened to come to town about halfway through my treatment," said Marcy. "He didn't seem surprised to see me at class. Afterwards when I went over to him, before I'd said a word, he told me I must keep up the good work." She shook her head. "How did he know what I was doing? I hadn't even told him."

"Seems you didn't need to."

Marcy nodded. "But it wasn't long before he was lecturing me again, warning me that the future was in my hands. It was all up to me. You know, after six weeks even my specialist was amazed. I hadn't lost a single hair over the treatment and hadn't ever felt sick. He showed me scans of where the tumor had been—there was only the smallest white dot left compared to what had been there before. I had to laugh—he asked me, straight out, whether I was doing something else. I just told him I sometimes imagined myself getting well. You know, there's no point talking to these people about mind–body stuff."

Following all this, delighted, I was shaking my head. "So that was it? No more treatment needed?"

"Clean bill of health!" she confirmed. "I only need to go back in six months' time for another check-up." "And the Medicine Buddha practice?"

"I'm still doing it two sessions a day. The third session I do a different meditation. When you go through an experience like I have," her eyes narrowed, "the practice *really* matters. And I've proved to myself it works. It's made me realize what Lama told me. It *is* all up to me. The future *is* in my mind. You know, there are people out there who've recovered from dread diseases from the power of their minds alone. They've made spontaneous recoveries."

"How come?"

"Do you know that cancer tumors, just like the organs of the body, are constantly regenerating? The cells of a tumor are continually dying and being replaced. It's not the same lump of matter that grows from the start. If you can address the intelligence that directs the energies in your body, and interrupt the 'instructions' to a tumor to regenerate, then the tumor must disappear. At some deep level I don't yet understand, rebalancing the body's energies is at the heart of Medicine Buddha practice."

Why things happen: The three models

"But Marcy, you've been meditating for years," I had to say. "You must wonder why you got cancer in the first place."

"Of course!" Her face was animated. "At first it was 'poor little me,' and I asked my specialist, and he started lecturing me on free radicals and cancer cells getting out of control and I just said, 'No! No! That's *how* you get cancer, not why.' Thing is," she put a hand on my arm, "I knew what the why was. *You* know what the why was."

"I do?"

Knocking back the rest of her champagne, Marcy got off the sofa and headed for the ice bucket. "There are only three possible explanations for why things happen." She stood, bottle in hand, as behind her in the darkness pleasure craft cruised up and down the lamp-lit Thames. This was Marcy in her element—champagne in hand and, best of all, an audience.

"Possibility number one—God. He makes things, or lets things happen. But when I look around the world today, I see no evidence of the hand of God. Not an all-mighty, all-loving God. Why would he let the Holocaust happen? Half a century later that still makes no sense. Why are black kids in Africa born with HIV, both parents dying of AIDS in six months? I don't buy that suffering makes you more compassionate when you're only two weeks old! And what about a snared antelope? An abusive stepfather? There are millions of things going on all the time that most people, even with only human-size compassion, wouldn't let happen if they could stop them.

"Possibility number two is chance. You know, everything

happens at random." She returned to the sofa and fixed me with a wry smile. "I don't know about you, but when I drive down the freeway, cows don't fly into my windshield. Cups of cappuccino don't spontaneously turn into champagne. Things don't just happen for no reason—that's not how things operate. Which is why the third possibility is the only one that makes sense to me."

"Karma?"

"Exactly. Cause and effect. What goes around, comes around."

I nodded. "I think I'm about to learn all about that next week."

It was Marcy's turn to look curious.

As she raised her glass to her lips, I took a sip of my own before telling her, "I've been going to this place called the Glebe Street Gompa . . ."

4. Karma

HE LAW OF CAUSE and effect, or karma, is a typically Buddhist concept—apparently simple but with profound consequences for the way we live. This much became apparent when I returned to the Glebe Street Gompa after Marcy's visit for another of Rinpoche's classes.

By now more familiar with gompa etiquette and class routine, I was also starting to recognize the faces of some of my fellow students. They were a welcoming lot, relaxed, lighthearted, and it was obvious that some of them knew each other well, discussing retreats they'd been to in the past. What, I wondered, were they doing at a Lam Rim course when they had presumably heard all these teachings before?

It was only later that I came to appreciate the difference between knowing something intellectually and understanding it from the heart. As with falling in love, no amount of hypothetical conjecture can substitute for personal experience. Endless hours watching TV soaps, or listening to heart-wrenching love songs on the radio, are no preparation at all for that first giddying wonderment of romantic intimacy. It is the same with Buddhism, where the most advanced theoretical understanding is considered altogether secondary to direct personal experience.

And just as romance is unlikely to blossom if you shut yourself away in your bedroom, so too it would be most unusual for realizations of ancient Buddhist wisdom to strike while you are propping up the local bar. There are no aspirants in Buddhism too advanced not to benefit from listening to the main teachings again—and again. Sometimes you have to hear a concept explained for the hundredth time before the light goes on.

"Today's lesson is about karma," Rinpoche had begun, looking about the class with his trademark mischievous smile. "'Karma' is a Sanskrit word which, strictly speaking, means 'action.' But what follows from action is a result. A consequence. Which is why we talk about the law of cause and effect.

"All of us take this law for granted in our daily lives. Every time we put our car key in the ignition, every time we boot up our computer, every time we switch on the kettle, we do so expecting a result. Well," he grinned, "maybe not every time we boot up the computer!

"The whole world operates according to cause and effect. Check up and you'll see. It doesn't matter if it's something as big as planetary climatic patterns, like El Niño, or as small as microbacterial activity; nothing happens by chance. There's a direct relationship between cause and effect."

He paused, regarding us seriously before saying slowly, "It's the same with mind. Every thought we have, every word we say, every action we take, creates a cause. Over a period of time, all these karmic causes ripen to become effects."

Buddhism frequently talks of a mindstream rather than mind, and it is true that the way we experience our mind is not as a fixed entity but as a constant flow of consciousness, clarity, and awareness. Into this flow, our actions predispose us to experience future events in particular ways, whether positive or negative. There is a stream of consciousness coursing through our life. Moment by moment, we are constantly shaping our karmic destiny.

The ultimate self-development program

Cognitive psychologists recognize that beliefs shape attitudes which in turn shape behavior. Self-development gurus from Norman Vincent Peale to Anthony Robbins have made fortunes from propagating this ancient but powerful truth. They point out that very frequently it isn't circumstance that's trapping us in a particular job, lifestyle, or relationship—it's our own self-limiting beliefs. Replace those "I can't" beliefs with "I can," and new vistas open up.

In his outstanding bestseller, *Awaken the Giant Within*, Anthony Robbins provides countless examples of sportspeople, musicians, and businesspeople who've reached their peak performance only when they changed their underlying beliefs about themselves.

I often think that Buddhism might be described as the ultimate self-development program. Personal wealth, an affluent lifestyle, career success, and status just weren't big enough goals for Buddha, who was, in any case, born wealthy and privileged. Buddha wasn't against wealth—on the contrary, money and power can achieve far more, at least in conventional terms, than poverty and powerlessness. But Buddha regarded the materialistic goals of a single individual as just too small, too short term, to be worthy of a lifetime's efforts.

Geshe Loden, head of the Tibetan Buddhist Society, talks about our "sesame seed minds," how we have a strong tendency to focus much of our attention only on our own material well-being in this particular lifetime. Even birds do that, says Geshe-la. Even insects! Surely as human beings we should be aiming a little bit higher?

How much more worthy would it be to abandon a sesame seed-size aspiration and choose a goal which encompasses not just our material well-being but also genuine inner happiness? Not just for ourselves, but for all others? Not just for this lifetime, but for all eternity?

"The good thing about the law of karma," said Rinpoche, "is that we have it in our power to create the causes for whatever effects we wish. A lot of Western people wrongly think that karma equals fate, or predestination. They think it's something you don't have any power to change. This is a misunderstanding. It is we who create our own karma and we can change it in a powerful, dynamic way. We are creating hundreds, even thousands, of such causes every day of our lives. But unless we have good mindfulness we may not even be aware of it. Once again we see how important it is to subdue our mad monkey minds, to be fully present in each moment.

"You see, it's not only the big things we do that matter. We don't have to do anything as dramatic as defraud our employers, or write a large check to a charity, to create negative or positive karma. Both of those actions, like all others, began as ideas in our minds, so that it is here, in our minds, that karma arises.

"We all tend to have habitual thoughts, or attitudes, and we need to be very careful about these. Often they build up, and have a cumulative effect which is immense. As Buddha said in the *Dharmapada*:

> The thought manifests as the word;
> The word manifests as the deed;
> The deed develops into habit;
> And habit hardens into character;
> So watch the thought and its ways with care,
> And let it spring from love born out of concern
>   for all beings . . .
> As the shadow follows the body,
> As we think so we become.

"If we want to know how our life will be in the future, we should look at how we think and act today. We are the sum total of the decisions we make. Or, to quote the Dalai Lama, 'Our present condition is not something causeless nor is it something caused by chance. It is something we ourselves have steadily constructed through our series of past decisions and the actions of body, speech, and mind that arose from them.'"

Our mindstream: Our choice

Earlier, we looked at the example of the two drivers who have to brake suddenly to allow another car to cut in. In one case the driver rants and raves at the selfish idiot in front of him. In the other the driver is unperturbed, continuing to hum along to the car radio.

The point I was making was that the causes of anger—and indeed every other response—are not out there in the world, as we generally assume them to be. They are present in our mind-stream, in the form of karma waiting to ripen. The indignant driver, by reacting with anger has—congratulations!—just created the cause to experience anger again. He may very well not realize that's what he's done. He almost certainly didn't plan to get angry. But until he is able to subdue his mind, in perpetuating this unhappy cycle he will continue to generate countless causes for his own future unhappiness.

This aspect of karma is significant in revealing that we are the authors of our own future happiness or misery. Even in the most desperate circumstances, we still have the opportunity to create limitless positive or negative karma. The small-business owner going through bankruptcy. The middle-aged wife whose husband leaves her for a younger woman. Even the forty-something man struck down with a life-threatening illness—all these people still have a choice in the attitude they adopt, which will determine their future experiences. Embitterment, recrimination, and self-pity may be understandable responses. But all that these would achieve, in karmic terms, would be to create the causes for still further unhappiness in the future. By contrast, through ridding ourselves of our me-focused attitude, the most traumatizing adversity can be faced with far greater equanimity than would otherwise be possible. Personal tragedy can actually be transformed to become a cause for limitless future happiness.

The inspiring example of Alison Davis is an illustration of this principle. Born with spina bifida, and having also to endure all the pain of a twisted spine, the Englishwoman defied statistics to survive into adulthood and marry. After her husband of ten years left her, the battle against pain became even harder, and she attempted suicide several times. Her medical condition, she knew, could only ever deteriorate. Paralyzed from the waist down and with no feeling in the right side of her body, she also suffered from emphysema and osteoporosis. What happiness could she ever find in her life?

In 1991 she was invited to sponsor two disabled children in India. She agreed, and four years later made the long and difficult journey to visit them. What she discovered appalled her—hundreds of disabled Indian children dumped by families who couldn't or wouldn't care for them. Alison's reaching out to help others marked a major turning point in her life. Returning to England, she set up a charity to raise money for these children. Enable (Working in India) has gone on to raise funds for the Alison Davis Home for Disabled Children, now a significant organization. It has given hope to many children who had none—and in so doing has also given Alison a sense of deep fulfillment. Alison's charity currently supports 347 disabled children, as well as fifteen students who were previously part of the program and have gone on to study at a college or university.

We don't have to look far to find other examples of people who are able to rise above personal tragedy to help others. Looking around our own communities, we very often find that those at the forefront of philanthropic activities have not had easy lives themselves, but have worked through the negativity to create the causes for happiness.

An empowering psychology

Karma is a challenging subject, because it turns upside down the idea that all our joys and despairs arise from what happens in the world around us. But it is ultimately a more empowering psychology than the one most of us take for granted, because it offers us the chance to transform our whole experience of reality.

One of the refreshing things about Buddhism, however, is its insistence that you should only take up those practices which benefit you. If certain aspects aren't helpful, simply put them to one side. You can always come back to them later. You won't go to hell because you don't believe in karma. Nor will believing in it guarantee you a place in heaven—like everything else in Buddhism, it is what you *do* that counts, not what you say you believe.

The questioning reader may, at this point, be wondering exactly what is meant by a karmic cause. We might admire those who work hard to create the causes for their own success. But if sheer determination and hard work are apparently not enough to guarantee it, what is?

Karma and conditions

What a man sows, this he will reap.

St. Paul's *Letter to the Galatians*, 6:7

It is significant that St. Paul, and Buddha before him, used the same analogy of planting seeds when talking about the future. It is a good analogy not only because of the direct association between cause and effect, but because of other implied factors which come into play. Buddhists describe these other factors as conditions.

In order for a seed to germinate and grow to be a healthy plant, it requires soil, moisture, and sunshine. Similarly, karma needs the right conditions if it is to ripen. An obvious enough point, so it is strange that we should have a tendency to confuse seeds with conditions. In our quest to rearrange the external circumstances of our lives, we are quite frequently like a farmer who lavishes the very best soil conditioner and fertilizers on his land, installs a state-of-the-art irrigation system, and expectantly awaits an abundant crop even though he has failed to plant a single seed.

According to conventional wisdom, financial success is the product of hard work, a preparedness to take risks, and other such considerations. But we all know stories of people who've followed this formula, done all the right things, and whose ventures have ended not in wealth but in failure.

Why? Because all the conditions may have been right, but without the karmic seeds in place, success was never even a possibility.

The businessman who works fourteen-hour days in pursuit of riches, but is tight-fisted with family and friends, and crosses the road to avoid charity collectors is, from a karmic point of view, exactly like the farmer cultivating fertile fields but failing to plant a single seed.

The beautiful but self-absorbed young woman who treats her family like servants, her father like an ATM (withdrawals only), and who constantly bitches behind her friends' backs shouldn't be surprised to find herself "unlucky" in love, perhaps very much later in life, when she has lost her youthful bloom. What other result can she really expect?

Just as conditions alone will fail to yield a positive outcome, so too will seeds without appropriate conditions. Donating all our company's profits to charity before heading off to the golf course to wait for the checks to come rolling in is not, regrettably, a formula for success—or we'd all be doing it.

Seeds plus conditions is the approach we need to adopt in seeking karmic results. It's an approach which resonates with many people, on both the rational and intuitive levels. But even then, why is it that the most exclusive suburbs of the world's major cities aren't populated entirely by our most generous, patient, and ethical fellow citizens?

Why bad things happen to good people

We may know karmic farmers who not only tend to conditions but are punctilious about planting seeds as well. An entrepreneur who not only runs a thriving business but who is also involved in a handful of charities. The charming and attractive society hostess who lavishes affection on all she encounters, especially supporting the old and needy.

Then something nasty happens. The entrepreneur's highly geared company is hit by a sales slump, leaving him with the humiliating prospect of bankruptcy. The society hostess discovers she has married a fraudster, who dumps her, having systematically looted her assets. Why, in short, do bad things happen to good people—and good things to bad people?

Buddhism accounts for this on the basis that just as our current moment of consciousness is part of a far greater mental continuum, so too our current life should be seen as part of a much bigger picture. In fact, our mindstream is seen as having existed, not since birth or even conception, but since beginningless time. If we were to view this particular life as a bead on a string, it would be only the last in a row of innumerable beads that stretches far beyond our eyesight, and comprehension, to infinity.

Whether we are born in good conditions or bad ones, and

what experiences we will live through in this life, is determined by the karma ripening in our mindstream. A seed that may have been planted two lifetimes ago can ripen to produce an effect which may have no bearing at all on our current behavior. Which is why the entrepreneur hits the sales slump and the society hostess finds herself alone and in penury.

While karma explains the dynamics by which we can consciously set out to create our own destiny, it can also be a very uncomfortable notion. What is the state of our karmic bank account? What horrors have we inflicted on others, in previous lifetimes, for which we have yet to suffer? Wouldn't it be so much nicer to believe in a more benevolent theory which absolves us of all responsibility for the consequences of our own harmful thoughts, speech, and actions?

However sobering the implications, the critical point is that our karma is subject to constant change. Because our mindstream is dynamic, so too are the karmic seeds being planted, and those coming to fruition through appropriate conditions will change from moment to moment. Buddhism offers powerful practices to purify negative karma and cultivate boundless positive karma. The inheritors of even the heaviest karmic debt have it within their power to achieve enlightenment within a single lifetime.

But in order to achieve this, we have first to take responsibility for ourselves and for our own destiny.

Karma and the blame culture

Never has the notion of personal responsibility been under siege as much as it is today. In a me-obsessed culture, the rights of the individual dominate to the extent that accepting personal responsibility is not only increasingly rare, it is even considered politically incorrect.

When a sixteen-year-old girl drops out of school to have a baby, how often is it claimed that she is the victim of depressed socioeconomic circumstances, and shouldn't be blamed for following dysfunctional role models? The husband of the wife who has an affair is blamed for spending too much time at the office. The doctor who performed life-saving heart surgery on an obese patient is sued for a complication which leaves his patient paralyzed in the left hand.

Suggestions that the sixteen-year-old need not have slavishly followed negative role models—not everyone does—or that the wife should have found a less duplicitous way to fill her leisure hours, or that the doctor should have been thanked for saving the life of someone who has already harmed himself are not always greeted with enthusiasm. It is as though sociologists have given us permission to attach responsibility for our own actions to other people and circumstances.

Buddhism takes the opposite view. "All blame lies in one," wrote the Buddhist sage Geshe Chekawa. This is a definitive statement of personal responsibility. Not only do we have it within our power to generate a mindstream that experiences events in a particular way—like the example of the two drivers—the kind of life we are experiencing is also entirely of our own making. In the words of Buddha:

> The infinite variety of beings and universes
> Has been created by the mind.
> All universes and beings are the result of karma.

Being generous for selfish reasons

Acceptance of the law of cause and effect invariably has the most transformative effect on our lives. In what is, for me, one of the most outstandingly ingenious aspects of Buddhist teachings, we come to realize that our own selfish interests lie in being altruistic. Just as the flowering of the lotus transcends the filth of the swamp, so too is it that those of us who normally think only of ourselves start to behave in a way that gives rise to outcomes far beyond our imagination.

If we want to be rich, it is in our own selfish interest to be generous. If we aspire to be good looking—at least in the next life, even if we have given up on this one!—then we should cultivate patience. Similarly, it is in our own self-focused best interest to maintain strict ethics, because in doing so we are maximizing our own future happiness and peace of mind.

The more mindful we become of our thoughts and behavior, the more alert we will be to the opportunities to cultivate causes for future positive effects. When people come knocking at the door collecting for charity, instead of resenting them we become grateful for an opportunity to enjoy future prosperity. Finding ourselves stuck in a bank line, we may out of habit react with irritation until we remember that we've just landed the chance to improve our whole demeanor. Provocative neighbors, demanding bosses, irksome spouses—we can see all these not only as arising from our own past actions, but also as providing the means for us to break out of self-defeating patterns of behavior.

Through the concept of karma we have an amazing way to turn around our automatic, negative experiences of people and situations. How can you really be angry with someone who is merely the instrument through which you are experiencing your own karma? It is like hating the stick you are being beaten with, rather than the force wielding it. How can you feel rage towards people who by their actions are condemning themselves to experiencing the same unhappiness that you are—and probably far worse?

Because Tibetan Buddhism is a living tradition, we don't have to look back thousands of years to find quite breathtaking examples of the transformative effects of karma. The monk Palden Gyatso was captured by the Chinese when they invaded Tibet in 1959, and jailed for thirty-three years, during which period he was subjected to brutal mental and physical torture, including vicious electric shock treatment. Eventually released, he fled to Dharamsala, in northern India, where he met the Dalai Lama. During this meeting, His Holiness asked about his experiences in jail. Having suffered to an extent most of us couldn't even begin to imagine, when asked what his worst experience had been, Palden Gyatso replied, "The fear that I would lose compassion for my jailers."

While we can only aspire to such a level of heroic selflessness, to have in our midst real-life examples of what can be achieved through Buddhist practices is immensely reassuring.

Months, years, or decades of being generous for selfish reasons begin to have a predictable effect. So habitual do our generosity, patience, and ethics become that their original cause—self-advancement—is left behind. The mask becomes the person. What starts out as a contrived and self-conscious change of attitude and behavior results in a genuine metamorphosis. Especially when combined with other practices, including various meditations, by mindfully exercising the law of karma we have it in our power not only to create the causes for repercussions way beyond this particular lifetime, but to achieve transformation within it. To reinvent ourselves, and our futures. To become, like Palden Gyatso, beings of infinite love and compassion.

"I'll be happy when . . ."

Don't overlook small and seemingly insignificant negative actions.
The smallest of sparks can burn down a mountain.

TIBETAN SAYING

Thinking about karma as a serious possibility, it's perhaps inevitable that you start by applying it to your own life. I certainly did. The recent ups and downs of my career still fresh in my mind, I couldn't help trying to remember any instances when I, like the former difficult colleague of my short-lived agency appointment, might have been particularly overbearing and unpleasant, thereby creating the causes for my subsequent unhappiness. But given that my job as a freelancer had turned out to be so much more rewarding than the high-flying career job, had the cause to encounter my obnoxious colleague actually arisen from some particularly good karma I had created in the past?

Then of course there was my great, unfulfilled ambition in life—to be a published writer. With ten unpublished novels behind me, it was now apparent that while I might have created the right conditions for publication, the karmic seeds just hadn't been there. I'd worked hard at it, but so what? I hadn't got my break. Then again, how many breaks had I given others?

Perhaps if I had gone out of my way to help friends and

acquaintances find jobs, or clients, or pursue their worldly aims in whatever ways they sought, then I too would be further on. I'd spent so much of the past decade shut away behind my desk, telling myself that by persistence and working at my craft I was sure to succeed. But perhaps if I'd written just six novels, instead of ten, and had spent some of that self-focused writing time working for the success of others, then enough karmic seeds would have been planted to have borne fruit.

Such are the imponderables of karma. Little did I know, even as I was considering them, that my writing karma was on the brink of major change.

Getting what you want

To my great surprise and delight, the book proposal I had mailed out to various publishers elicited not just one, but three expressions of interest. Not that I allowed myself to get my hopes up. I'd discussed ideas with editors several times in the past to no avail. There is a vast difference between an interested chat and a publishing contract. Besides, as a freelancer, my attention was now caught up in all sorts of more imminent projects.

But one Friday afternoon came the phone call for which in some ways I felt I had been waiting my whole adult lifetime. An editor from one of the major publishers said she'd like to publish *The Invisible Persuaders*.

I was thirty-four years old and had been writing since I was eighteen. Ten books and one proposal later I was about to realize my most cherished and long-held dream. Within hours my wife, ever supportive, had arrived home clutching a bottle of Moët et Chandon. And after a night of celebrations, the very next morning we made our way to Burlington Arcade in Piccadilly, where she bought me the pen I had always promised myself if I ever reached this definitive moment: a Mont Blanc Meisterstuck Legrand.

Many people have their own private symbols and touchstones. Now I had mine and, I felt, I could *really* call myself a writer.

Friends and family responded to the news with great excitement. Knowing how long I'd been working towards this goal, they understood how much it meant to me. There were several "drink and dial" sessions, as my wife refers to them, to friends back home in Africa. Yes, all my friends agreed, this was fabulous news!

A week or two after the initial celebrations, I was struck by how little had actually changed. I still had to get out of bed every morning in the cold and the dark. I still did the same work for the same clients. The advance I was to be paid for the book was only a fraction of normal PR rates, if I looked at it from a time point of view, so I had to fit the writing around my usual consultancy assignments.

Like many other people of a Calvinistic background, I am something of an expert in the self-defeating art of postponed happiness. "I will be happy when X, Y, or Z happens" is the general gist of things. When I get the job, the lover, the car. In my case it was, "When I get the book deal my cup will runneth over with great joy and happiness." At that moment, according to the Maslow theory of the hierarchy of needs, my self-actualization would become complete. So where was the long-awaited, often-promised, "sixteen years in the making" great joy and happiness? Why was it that I felt so . . . well, normal? Why wasn't I romping across Wandsworth Common singing "The Hills Are Alive with the Sound of Music"?!

There is a scene in a *Fawlty Towers* episode where one of the guests complains about the view from her hotel window. The ever-exasperated Basil Fawlty, gesturing out the window, demands, "What did you expect from a window in Torquay? Herds of wildebeest stampeding across the plains? The Hanging Gardens of Babylon?"

I am not sure what it was, exactly, I'd expected to feel with a book contract under my belt, but it was certainly different from what I was experiencing. Only later I came across the famous aphorism of George Bernard Shaw, to which I could instantly relate: "There are two disappointments in life; not getting what you want, and getting it."

My mistake, of course, was to expect an external event to make me happy to a degree that was never going to happen. Delighted as I was to land a publishing contract, it didn't change everything. I discovered that I had attached all kinds of expectations to this event which, when it finally occurred, failed to materialize. The same could be said for any career ambition: making it to partnership, taking home a bonus of $X thousand, securing a particularly prestigious and lucrative client. Against all experience, we have this capacity to keep deluding ourselves that the achievement of some particular milestone will represent a major personal breakthrough. But after sometimes the shortest of honeymoons we wake up one morning and discover we're still just us.

A new beginning

Over the next eight months the book got written. After copious desk research, interviews, and drafting, a typescript emerged. *The Invisible Persuaders*, subtitled *How Britain's Spin-*

doctors Manipulate the Media, focused, as one would expect, on some of the more dubious practices in the world of PR. These ranged from a trivial form of deception used by some London practitioners, whereby newspaper coverage is photocopied at 115 percent to give clients the impression a larger piece of newspaper has been occupied, to the far more sinister practice of circulating among journalists anonymous but highly damaging "intelligence" about corporate enemies.

The libel reading that followed turned out to be almost as exhausting as writing the book itself. Never having had to work with a libel lawyer up until that point, I came to discover that it's not good enough simply to know that something under-handed has happened—you have to be able to prove it in black and white. As a result of the endless legal questions, which ran to over thirty pages of bullet points, I had to excise a number of the juicier details from my book. The key stories survived, but in neutered form. Despite this, I did feel I was working towards achieving an important goal, and one to which my still very basic dharma practice had contributed in two important ways. The first, already mentioned, was the new clarity with which I had been able to identify an opportunity which might other-wise have eluded me. The second was the nonattachment with which I'd made my pitch to publishers.

It is one of life's curious paradoxes that the goals to which we have greatest attachment are most likely to escape us, while those we don't care so much about just fall into our laps. This phenomenon, taught by trainers of salespeople, was reinforced for me when I watched a TV documentary on wealthy entre-preneurs giving their views on why they had succeeded. The one that has always stuck in my mind was a British magazine magnate speaking from the poolside of his Caribbean home, resplendent in gold chains and sunglasses, piña colada in hand. "The important thing is not to care too much if you win or lose," he declared. "I'm always putting deals up, but the truth is, I don't really give a damn."

In that same spirit of clear-sightedness and not being too attached to outcomes, once my typescript had finally made it past the scrutiny of both the libel lawyer and a particularly zealous proofreader, I found myself wondering what to do next. The gestation period in book publishing is agonizingly long. During the period between a novelist handing in a completed typescript, and its eventual publication, it's not unusual for the author to have written one or more books, so that by the time the first carefully crafted story finally does hit the bookshelves the author can barely remember the names of the main characters.

For my part, I didn't have a new book to work on. And while my PR consultancy work kept me both interested and occupied, the eventual publication of *The Invisible Persuaders* would not, I hoped, be a once-only event.

Having been driven to write fiction since an early age, my thoughts naturally strayed back in this direction. As much as I'd enjoyed writing *The Invisible Persuaders*, there could be no denying that the libel elimination process had stripped the book of its more eyebrow-raising revelations. The power of exposés often lies as much in the revealing, authenticating details as in the overarching tale of duplicity. The design of the underwear worn by a member of Parliament during his extramarital trysts seems to be of as much interest as the adultery itself. The bottle of Chianti enjoyed as an evil genius tucks into his flambéed human liver seems as intriguing as the act of cannibalism. It was precisely these kinds of details that had to be excluded from *The Invisible Persuaders*. What a relief it would be to have the legal brakes off! And how much more true an account could be revealed in so-called fiction! So was born the idea of the PR thriller.

Once again, I was taking nothing for granted. Devising a proposal, I wrote a few sample chapters and wrote a bullish letter to one of London's most high-profile agents, alerting him to the upcoming publication of *The Invisible Persuaders*. I was naturally pleased when he agreed to take me on as a client, but I wasn't getting too excited; I'd been taken on before without success. The idea this time was that my new agent would use the buzz which we hoped would accompany the publication of *Persuaders* as the context in which to interest potential editors in my "debut" novel.

The launch of *The Invisible Persuaders* was held at the Conrad Hotel, in Chelsea Harbour, on a glorious June day. Janmarie and I had decided to do something different from the usual evening drinks and canapés, opting instead for a champagne brunch. It was wonderful to be joined by close friends and family to celebrate the realization of such a long-held dream, and especially in such lavish surroundings. Even the weather rose to the occasion; outside, balmy blue skies and sunshine formed an almost Mediterranean backdrop to the opulent yachts tugging at their moorings.

Exactly ten years before, I had arrived in what seemed to be a sprawling, bewildering city to become a published writer—and finally it had happened. Along the way I had met and married my wonderful Australian wife, I'd become a Londoner, and had advanced much further in my PR career than I would have thought possible. As for my meditation practice, it was still in its very early days, but it had become an important part of my life, and I sensed it would become still more so.

Perhaps events of the recent past had given me the confidence to be even more adventurous. Or perhaps ten years of English winters and feeling constantly worn down by the inescapable combination of traffic congestion, bad public transportation, sky-high property prices, and pollution of every kind made me yearn for the wide open spaces and sunshine of my early life. Whatever the cause, Janmarie and I uncharacteristically threw caution to the wind and decided on a complete change. We rented out our flat. Bought a round-the-world ticket. And with no fixed agenda, made our way first to the USA, then on to Australia.

Would my agent succeed in selling my "first" novel? Would we return to live in London, or find a new home somewhere else? Would my meditation practice survive several months of travel? As we packed our bags for New York, I didn't know the answers to any of these questions. But nor was I particularly concerned. We would take the future one day at a time, and allow events to unfold.

As it happened, even in the short term, my experiences were beyond what I would ever have dared to imagine.

5. This Precious Life

*It probably has been many lifetimes since we have had such
an auspicious conjunction of conditions favorable
to progress along the path to higher being.*

THE DALAI LAMA

WHILE MY JOURNEY to become both a published writer and self-employed PR consultant hadn't been easy, massive rejection is as much a feature of life as an author as workplace conflicts are of life in the corporate world. More to the point is that in hindsight, with the benefit of the Dharma, I realize that I made things very much harder for myself than I needed to. Eager as I was to fulfill dreams which, in truth, amounted to nothing more than an all too conventional rearranging of the externals, I had been missing a much bigger point. In fact the teachings I received on this precious life in my last weeks in London made me wonder how I could have achieved so little of real value.

There is a chapter in the Lam Rim, discussing the preciousness of human life, which many editions translate as "Leisure and Fortune." When I first saw the heading my instant reaction was, "Great! Some secret Tibetan wisdom on how to get massively rich." Clearly, the magazine magnate sipping his piña colada at the poolside of his Caribbean villa still loomed large in my subconscious mind—such is the power of attachment!

The curious thing about the Leisure and Fortune teachings, however, is that by the end of them I felt so lucky I might just as well have been that multi-millionaire.

From a Buddhist perspective you, the reader of this book, and I, the writer, are among the all-time greatest winners in the lottery of life. We rank among a tiny percentage of the most fortunate beings to have ever lived. The conditions we enjoy put us in a category of dazzlingly good karma that is truly breathtaking.

Most of the time, of course, we seldom feel that way. Swamped by images of other people's affluence, influence, sex appeal, and celebrity, and with massively powerful advertising industries charging our aspirations still further, it's easy to feel that we're little more than an also-ran in the great rat race of life. Playing a bit part. A minor role. No matter how much we've achieved, it's easy to think of plenty of others who've achieved much more.

So how is it that Buddhism comes to such a different conclusion?

According to Buddhist cosmology, the two modes of existence we are aware of—animal and human—are by no means the only realms in existence. Like other great spiritual traditions, Buddhism contends there are a variety of hell realms, spirit realms, and deva realms, with animals and humans about two-thirds of the way up the food chain. Like any food chain, the numbers get proportionately smaller the higher you go, so that the beings in the hell realms greatly outnumber those in the spirit realms, which in turn outnumber animals, humans, and so on.

For those readers who find it hard to accept the possible existence of a realm that can't be detected through our senses, unreliable as those senses may be, even if we consider ourselves in the context of the observable animal and human realms we can grasp the significance of our immense good fortune.

Buddhism uses the term "sentient being," referring to the Tibetan word *sem-chen* meaning "having mind." All sentient beings are equal in wanting to enjoy happiness and avoid suffering. As all pet owners know, animals' likes and dislikes are just as particular as our own and in some cases not much different. Enjoyable meals, warmth, companionship and a nice place to relax are just a few of our shared objectives, but how many animals ever come close to realizing their most basic needs?

We are increasingly receiving fresh insights into the sentience of nonhumans—about which most people are in varying degrees of denial. The abilities of chimpanzees to use modified computers to communicate thoughts and feelings should prompt questions about our use of these intelligent creatures in laboratories, especially in experiments of dubious value. Stories of how pet pigs have woken their owners in the middle of the night, alerting them to a fire which would otherwise have killed them, and other such evidence, may make us question how we can subject these same animals to the horror of the abattoir.

Scientist Rupert Sheldrake has documented numerous experiments, as well as a large volume of anecdotes, confirming that many animal species possess a higher level of intelligence and feelings than we generally assume. In the absence of human forms of communication, their telepathic skills can also be outstanding (as revealed in books such as *Dogs That*

Know When Their Owners Are Coming Home and *The Sense of Being Stared At)*.

Many people avoid thinking about the sentience of animals, perhaps because of the ethical dilemma it presents next time they order a hamburger, or perhaps because they are simply in denial about evidence that animals do think and feel. But as research continues in this area, attitudes are likely to change. In the words of Arthur Schopenhauer, the German philosopher, "First, it is ridiculed. Second, it is violently opposed. Finally, it is accepted as self-evident."

Despite our shared desires for happiness and to avoid suffering, the bleak reality is that most beings on this planet exist as nothing more than food for others. From the tiny plankton to the mighty whale, most ocean-dwellers live under constant threats to their lives. On land the story isn't much different. Whether wildlife, under remorseless attack from other animals and poachers, or domesticated sheep and cattle, bred in their billions for the slaughterhouse, the simple truth is that for most sentient beings, life on earth is a desperately threatened mode of existence. For many millions it is more brutal and terrifying than we ever allow ourselves to contemplate, given our personal and direct responsibility for so much of that brutality and terror. Had we any inkling of the agonies being experienced right now, at this very moment, as animals are being slaughtered by slow barbaric methods, or having needles plunged into their bile ducts, or being torn to pieces by predators, the experience would be overwhelming.

Those minorities of animals spared the sufferings of their peers may have the good fortune to live more contented lives. But even the most pampered Manhattan pooch has only the most limited ability to create positive causes for future positive effects; intellectually and karmically challenged, what hope does it have of achieving anything meaningful in its lifetime?

Our "average" life

From the countless trillions of animals, when we move up a realm to the six and a half billion humans, what we find, according to various analyses by the United Nations, is sobering to say the least:

- 2.5 billion people live on less than $2 a day. Put another way, 40 percent of the world's population receives only 5 percent of its income.
- A cow in the European Union "earns" more than most people in Africa, its owners receiving a daily $2.20 subsidy, while 75 percent of Africans live on less than $2 a day.
- At the current rate, it will take more than 130 years to rid the world of hunger.
- Every hour more than 1,200 children, in the world's poorest countries, die from preventable diseases.
- Today, someone living in Zambia has less chance of reaching age 30 than someone born in England in 1840.
- In India, the death rate for children age 1–5 is 50 percent higher for girls than for boys. Expressed differently, 130,000 children die each year because they are female. Next door in Pakistan, 2 million children miss out on the chance of education—because they are girls.
- Every year over 900,000 people, mainly women and children, become victims of people-trafficking.
- There are 100 million "missing" women who would be alive but for infanticide, neglect, and sex-selective abortions.

- 113 million school-age children are not in school—97 percent of them in developing countries.
- Of the world's 200 countries, only 82, with 57 percent of the world's population, are fully democratic.
- 61 countries, with 38 percent of the world's population, still do not have a free press.

Behind this list of cold statistics lies an immensity of human suffering which most of us can't begin to imagine. Many of us, probably most readers of this book, would define themselves as living pretty average or "middle-class" lifestyles, which may be true in terms of the society in which we live. What we overlook is that the majority of our fellow humans have no access to the developed-world benefits we take utterly for granted. "Average" income levels, education and health systems, law and order and democracy, which we regard as normal, are, in reality, extremely abnormal. By any objective measurement, our "normal" existence constitutes a life of overwhelming privilege. Being middle class in a First World country in reality means to live among the luckiest top 10 percent of the human population, and to enjoy leisure and fortune of a kind that the 90 percent can only ever dream about.

In this context, the desire to move from among the top 10 percent to the top 8 percent, by getting our hands on a bigger home, car, or stock portfolio, seems rather like a lottery winner arguing that he should be paid $556 million instead of $554 million. We're already hands-down winners on the most spectacular scale. Wanting even more seems positively ungracious!

The rarity of Buddhist wisdom

If all this weren't enough, things get even more statistically unlikely when we consider a further aspect of "Leisure and Fortune" as defined by the Lam Rim: the opportunity to study Buddhist teachings. The high value that is placed on this arises from the recognition that without the mental technology offered by Buddhism, people are doomed to live under a number of interrelated delusions. Some of these have already been discussed, and others will follow. Examples include the belief that people and objects have intrinsic characteristics rather than the qualities we project onto them. The belief that people and objects have the capacity to bring us a happiness which will last a moment longer than our positive mental projections. The belief that we are just normal people going about our ordinary business, rather than beings so richly endowed with opportunity that, compared to most sentient beings, we lead a godlike existence.

It's true that most of these beliefs are implicit rather than explicit. But they are so deeply ingrained that most of us rarely stop to challenge them. Buddhist teachings are held to be extremely rare and precious because they provide the tools to break free of a fundamentally distorted view of reality, and the practices to seize control of our destiny way beyond this particular lifetime.

It is only very recently that Tibetan Buddhism has come to be known outside Tibet. Until twenty years ago there were very few translated texts, or even teachers. How many of the world's notional ten percent with leisure and fortune are also fortunate enough to be exposed to Buddhism—and have the karma to follow its practices? Probably only one in many thousands, meaning that those of us who are Buddhists are among the most minute fraction of a percentage point of the population. And that's just the human population. What if we were to include animals too? Not to mention sentient beings from other realms and an infinity of other planets? Just how lucky can one person be?!

Buddha illustrated this very point with an analogy:

> If there were a huge, deep ocean as big as this entire
> world with a golden yoke floating on its surface, and,
> at the bottom, there was a crippled, blind turtle who
> surfaced only once in a hundred years, how often
> would that turtle raise its head through the yoke?
> (*Sutra Containing the Excellent*)

Such an event would be extremely rare, said Buddha, but not as rare as gaining a human life of leisure and fortune.

The Dr. Faustus in me

All the time we spend fretting about our jobs, our frustrated ambitions, our petty domestic irritations seems somehow obscene in light of this analysis. We have a life of leisure and fortune so unbelievably precious, and what do we do with it? For the most part, if we're honest, not much of ultimate value.

Christopher Marlowe's famous play *Dr. Faustus* tells the story of an ambitious Renaissance doctor who sold his soul to the devil in return for twenty-four years of supernatural powers. The central tragedy of the drama is that, having paid so highly for his abilities, once in possession of them the brilliant doctor achieves little of substance, descending instead to playing party tricks. At the end he is dragged to hell by demons, agonizing over how he could have squandered his future for so little.

How much like Dr. Faustus are we? In a rare position to advance our own mental development, to benefit both ourselves and others with relatively little effort, why is it that we focus so much of our energies on mundane preoccupations, and that the highest we generally set our sights is on sipping piña coladas in a Caribbean villa?

It's also worth considering how we came by this extremely rare opportunity: why are we among a tiny percentage of the most privileged beings on earth?

As outlined in the last chapter, the Buddhist perspective is that nothing happens by chance, and everything is driven by karma. The seeds for this precious life were planted at a previous time in our mindstream. The desire to give others happiness (love) or prevent their suffering (compassion) in the past was the karmic cause for our current life.

It is said that when Shakyamuni Buddha was in the hell realms, long before he became even a human, the moment he experienced compassion for a fellow inmate marked the start of his ascent to enlightenment.

If we wish, we have it in our power to ensure our own future, true happiness—along with health, wealth, and yes, even piña coladas. Nobody is stopping us from planting hundreds, even thousands of seeds on a daily basis, which can only ripen into positive effects. We don't have to throw in our jobs and become charity workers in the Third World to do this. We don't have to dump our spouses and children and retreat to the Himalayas. As already discussed in the last chapter, the challenges of everyday life are what provide us with our richest opportunities for the creation of happiness.

Our limitless opportunity

Most sentient beings have only the most limited opportunity to create positive karma and develop their minds. Their short lives characterized by fear and aggression, it is inevitable that the karma they create will be overwhelmingly negative.

We, on the other hand, have limitless opportunity to create positive causes, but how well do we fare? Looking at our actions of body, speech and mind on a day-by-day basis, how much of what we do is a cause for positive or negative future effects?

This precious life, one which only the tiniest proportion of sentient beings enjoy, presents us with a rare opportunity to break free altogether from the endless cycle of rebirth and suffering. It is up to us to make the most of it. If we don't, in the words of the Buddhist teacher Aryasurya:

Like a trader gone to an island of jewels

Returning home empty-handed,

Without the paths of the ten virtues

You will not obtain [a life of leisure and fortune] again in the future.

Our greatest teacher

Death holds very little hope for ordinary worldly persons with no spiritual experience . . . Control over one's future evolution is to be won during one's life, not at the time of death.

DALAI LAMA

A close friend of mine was blown up by a landmine at the age of eighteen. A soldier in the Rhodesian army, Jack's job had been to remove mines planted by ZANLA terrorists. On this particular occasion, the mine had been booby-trapped in an unexpected way. Lying on the ground only a short distance away, when the mine exploded he took the force of it down his left side.

Helicoptered to the hospital, for several days, during rare moments of consciousness, he believed he was going to die. Aware only that he was in hospital and had suffered major trauma, he was convinced he'd reached the end.

When Jack's condition stabilized, and consciousness returned more fully, he found himself with a bandage wrapped around his head; shrapnel had damaged both eyes. He was told he would be blind for the rest of his life.

As things turned out, Jack made a remarkable recovery, not only able to get up and about, but also regaining sufficient sight in one eye to enable him to do most things except drive at night. Just as remarkable, perhaps, was the impact of the explosion on his mindset. Pre-explosion Jack had been an intense, solitary individual who took life rather seriously. Post-explosion he became one of the most easygoing people you could hope to meet, a lively conversationalist always ready with a witty riposte. As students, when groups of us sat around drinking beer late into the night, Jack would be there at the heart of things, picking out the small pieces of Chinese-manufactured shrapnel which surfaced in his leg, and which he kept in a glass test tube on his desk—a macabre reminder of his life-changing experience.

Living each day as a bonus

The Sufis have a saying: "Die before you die and you shall never die". It is one I know Jack would endorse. Because once the threats of both death and permanent blindness had receded, he thought of the time he had ahead of him as an extraordinary stroke of luck. By all accounts he should have been killed, so he considered every day he lived afterwards as a bonus, a gift.

Jack's reaction to a very real encounter with death was not unique. Learning from the experiences of others who have recovered from apparently fatal heart attacks or terminal diseases, we find that they frequently emerge from the ordeal with a very different set of priorities from those they held before.

Faced with the reality of our own death, we quickly work out what really matters. More often than not, we discover that much of our life has been spent in pursuit of things of little lasting value. While it is too late to change what has already happened, it is never too late to change how you are in the present and the future. A privileged few, like Jack, have the benefit of the experience at the start of their adult lives, and live for many more years with the wisdom it brings.

It is for this reason that Buddhism emphasizes the importance of meditating on one's own death, not just as an occasional exercise, but as part of our daily practice. Some people's automatic reaction to this is that Buddhists must have some sort of morbid streak. Instead of accentuating the negative, they challenge, aren't there happier things to think about?

Paradoxically, no. As the cases of Jack and many others like him demonstrate, truly facing death makes us appreciate the preciousness of life. In the words of Buddha, "Just as the elephant's footprint is the biggest footprint on the jungle floor, death is the greatest teacher."

Our gaze averted

One of our challenges, as busy people, is to properly value each day that we live. Wrapped up as we are in our preoccupation with demanding jobs, our homes, families, and much-needed recreation, it often takes some dramatic intervention to awaken us to the reality that our lives dangle from the most slender of threads. Our continuation next year, next month, even tomorrow should never be automatically assumed.

But our tendency is to think of car accidents, medical emergencies, and other life-threatening crises as extraordinary, as though we should all live to a notional "average" lifespan of seventy or eighty-something, that we are safe from death until then.

The Buddhist view is that this approach is not only inaccurate, it's part of being in denial about death. Even though it is the one certainty of our lives, it's an issue we'd rather not think about. In the words of the much-loved American teacher, Lama Surya Das, "We are surrounded by death even if our gaze is averted."

Why do we do this?

People who believe we are nothing more than flesh and bone, and that when we die nothing continues, would say there is no point making yourself unhappy thinking about the prospect of your demise. But as Jack's case illustrates, even nihilists could get more out of life if confronting their own mortality made them wake up each morning with the real sense that "the next twenty-four hours are truly precious time."

Reminding ourselves that our lives are only temporary can also be effective in managing stress. For busy people, responsibilities and deadlines can combine to create a level of anxiety which acts like an acid, eating away our capacity for relaxation and enjoyment. The Buddhist emphasis on impermanence, however, provides a useful tool to counter this. By reminding ourselves that all the activities in which we're involved are only temporary, we get a better and more accurate perspective, and avoid feeling overwhelmed.

I have a friend who advocates that when you go to work you should imagine that you're just filling in for a friend that day. It's a once only experience and you'll do the best you can. But there's no need to plague yourself with "What if?" scenarios and other stress-inducing thoughts—it's only a temp job, right? Extending the logic, you get home not to your husband, wife, or partner, but to someone with whom you are having dinner. Ditto the kids you're babysitting. In the rented house.

Our life is an ongoing sequence of fleeting experiences. We only need to look back over the past five to ten years to see that. It's when we concretize things and make them feel permanent that we cause ourselves problems. Recognizing impermanence is wisdom not only of Buddhism, but of the Judeo-Christian and Islamic traditions too. It was exactly this motivation which was the reason for the inscription in King Solomon's gold ring, designed to help him appreciate the good times and get through the bad: "This, too, will pass."

The Queen and the kookaburra

Most of us who admit to unease about our postdeath future do so from fear of losing all that we know. What happens next?

As the Dalai Lama points out, "If we look around we can see we are enmeshed by suffering on every side. How can we expect similar conditions not to be present with us after the body dies? But then we have no wealth, power, friends, or even a body with which to protect ourselves."

In purely material terms, death is the great leveler. Geshe Loden has a phrase well understood, and often quoted by his students: "On the day she dies the Queen and the kookaburra will be the same." With no disrespect intended to Her Majesty, the simple fact is that, stripped of her body, wealth, status, and friendships, like a kookaburra that dies at the same time, the mindstreams of two beings will be all that remains. Both Queen and bird will experience themselves as clarity and awareness propelled by karma.

We too.

Shantideva gives a particularly acute insight:

> For though they get themselves a wealth of property,
> Enjoying reputation, sweet celebrity,
> Who can say where they have gone to now
> With all the baggage of their affluence and fame?

What has happened to the mindstreams of all those people who've dominated the headlines but are no longer with us? Members of the royal family, politicians, movie stars, business tycoons, rock chicks, and other celebrities—where are they now and what are they doing? Did they cultivate the massive positive karma needed for a precious human rebirth with leisure and fortune, or are they in a lower realm where positive karma is so much more difficult to accumulate? Is their mindstream now that of the bird perched in the tree outside your window? And what of our own mindstream—where is it headed?

The death process

The death process is a very important subject in Tibetan Buddhism, which provides a wealth of detailed instruction on the stages, or "bardos," of death, the intermediate stage, and rebirth. Sogyal Rinpoche's seminal work, *The Tibetan Book of Living and Dying*, provides enormously useful instruction for people facing their own deaths, or the deaths of those close to them.

For the purposes of an introductory book such as this it's enough to say that Buddhism teaches that life is best lived when founded not only on mindfulness of death, but also on mindfulness of our rare leisure and good fortune. We have, now, an opportunity enjoyed by only a fraction of a single percentage of human beings—let alone all beings. This opportunity will definitely come to an end, perhaps even later today. When it goes, unless we have created sufficient positive karma in our mindstream, who can tell what experiences we may have to endure?

While there is nothing intrinsically wrong with normal worldly pursuits like making money, bringing up families and enjoying recreation, it is also true that unless they are well motivated, the benefits of these activities are short-term. What an enormous tragedy it would be to squander a precious and necessarily limited opportunity, to achieve nothing of longer-term significance. As the Dalai Lama puts it, "We should not be like a beggar doing nothing meaningful year after year, ending up empty-handed at death."

Buddhism provides a sound basis on which to cultivate not only happiness in this present life but, in the longer term, nothing less than the great bliss of enlightenment. It also provides us with all the mental tools we need to proceed through the death process and the bardo state which follows it to ensure, at the very least, positive future rebirth. If we are particularly diligent, we have it within our means to achieve complete and final freedom from the endless cycle of uncontrolled rebirth and death.

Living examples

We know this to be true not on account of blind faith in texts or gurus, but because we are surrounded by beings in varying stages of mental evolution. The most developed of these beings have such mastery over their minds that their physical deaths are truly astonishing. In some cases the dying person's heart will stop beating and breathing will cease, but they will remain in a meditative posture for a period of several days, bodies glowing with health. In other cases, the homes of dying yogis have been found bathed in rainbow-colored light. Inside, instead of a corpse, all that is discovered is an ambrosial fragrance—together with a small bundle of hair and nails.

These are not ancient fables, but current happenings. They go unreported in the West because the communities in which they occur are usually in the East, have nothing to prove, and certainly no desire to turn the death of a loved one into a tabloid freak show. What's more, such occurrences have always been regarded as a normal, if infrequent, signal of special accomplishment in parts of India.

Some of the most compassionate of those highly evolved

ones have the ability to choose to return to live among us, to continue the work of their previous incarnation. The current Dalai Lama, for example, is recognized as the fourteenth incarnation of the same mental continuum which has returned in successive lifetimes to be the leader of Tibetan Buddhists.

But His Holiness is by no means alone. There are many other recognized reincarnations, or tulkus, who have chosen to be reborn in the West. One of the most famous is Lama Yeshe.

The example of Lama Yeshe

When the iron bird flies, and horses run on wheels, the Tibetan people will be scattered like ants across the World, and the Dharma will come to the land of red-faced people.

PADMASAMBHAVA (CIRCA A.D. 800)

Lama Thubten Yeshe was a pioneer in popularizing Buddhist teachings in the West, especially in America. A charismatic bridge-builder between East and West, he has been described by his friend, the author Vicki Mackenzie, as "round, warm, funny, at times outrageous, at times exquisitely touching, and always reaching out to us using whatever method he could to get his message across." A British journalist working for national newspapers, Mackenzie was among the first to write about the question of reincarnation for the general public. Her internationally bestselling book *Reincarnation: The Boy Lama* tells the story of the Spanish boy Ösel, who was recognized by the Dalai Lama as the reincarnation of her Tibetan teacher, Lama Thubten Yeshe.

Born in Tibet in 1935, from a very young age Lama Yeshe expressed a strong desire to lead a religious life. He loved visiting a nearby convent, attending Buddhist ceremonies, and whenever a monk came to the family home he would beg to be allowed to leave with him to join his monastery.

When he turned six, his parents allowed him to join Sera Je, a college at one of the three great Gelug monastic centers near Lhasa. In keeping with monastic tradition, there he stayed until the age of twenty-five, receiving teachings from a variety of high-ranking lamas in both the Lam Rim (sutra) and Vajyrayana (tantra) paths. Extensive memorization of texts, analysis, and vigorous debate have always been the hallmarks of Buddhist teaching, and Lama Yeshe was steeped in these by the time he left Sera Je.

In 1959, as he would sometimes put it, "the Chinese kindly told us that it was time to leave Tibet and meet the outside world." Escaping through Bhutan, he met up with other Tibetan refugees in northeast India where he continued his studies. There he also acquired his own heart-disciple, Thubten Zopa Rinpoche.

Origins of FPMT

It wasn't until the mid-1960s, when Lama Yeshe was thirty, that he had his first significant contact with Westerners. Requests for teachings from an American woman, Zina Rachevsky, saw Lama Yeshe and Lama Zopa move to Nepal. After a few years, they were able to purchase land at the top of a hill near Kathmandu called Kopan, where they founded the Mahayana Gompa Center in 1969. When the first meditation course was given there in 1971, it was attended by twenty students. By the time of the seventh course, in 1974, interest was so great the numbers had to be limited to 200!

Such was the modest beginning of the Foundation for the Preservation of the Mahayana Tradition (FPMT), now one of the most extensive Tibetan Buddhist organizations in the world. By the mid-1970s, having taught thousands of Western-ers, including pot-smoking hippies and earnest seekers who'd traveled to India to "find" themselves, it seemed inevitable that Lama Yeshe would begin traveling to the West to teach. Not only had his English improved, but so had his understand-ing of the Western mind. His presence was unlike anything most people had ever experienced; he radiated such love, com-passion and mischievous intelligence that students were fre-quently moved to tears by his words.

As Vicki Mackenzie puts it in *Reincarnation: The Boy Lama*:

> His answers were marvelous, somehow exactly what we needed. He completely demolished all our dualis-tic, narrow concepts. "Your Mickey Mouse minds! You are so boxed in, so narrow," he said. Some-how, his words were like a miracle. He spoke such utter common sense, made everything seem so sim-ple. Our confusion and worries simply dissolved away. He knitted everyone together, cut across all divisions.

Between the mid-1970s and 1984, Lama Yeshe traveled exten-sively to Europe, the UK, the USA, and Australia, creating an indelible impression on countless new students. Visiting Christian monasteries, taking to the Australian beaches for three days to learn about beach culture, and mingling with the crowds at Disneyland, he had no hesitation in abandoning traditional Tibetan customs to learn more about his students. And he was invariably accompanied by Lama Zopa, who provided an ascetic counterbalance to his irrepressible extrovertism. So when the much-loved lama died of a heart condition in Los Angeles, in early 1984, his passing sent waves of shock and sadness right around the world. He was only forty-nine years old.

Lama Yeshe had been seriously ill for four months, although according to Western medical reports since 1974 it was a miracle that he was alive at all. Two valves in his heart were faulty and because of the enormous amount of extra work it had to do to pump blood, the heart had enlarged to about twice its normal size. He himself had said ten years before that he was alive "only through the power of mantra."

It was now up to Lama Zopa, his faithful student, to oversee arrangements. These began with a vigil at Cedars Sinai Hospital in Los Angeles. Like many highly realized masters, Lama Yeshe's physical death was followed by two days in a meditative state before a final, subtle movement of his head signaled a successful transference of consciousness. Later his body was cremated at Boulder Creek, Colorado.

The new beginning

On 12 February 1985, in Granada, Spain, Ösel Hita Torres was born to parents Maria and Paco. The new baby was unplanned, and initially, as far as Maria was concerned, not entirely welcome. The couple already had four children under six years of age in an overcrowded house. Paco, a builder, had been underemployed for quite some months and the family was seriously in debt.

An ordinary family living in the village of Bubión in southern Spain, perhaps the only unusual thing about the Hita Torreses was their interest in Tibetan Buddhism. In 1977 they had attended a two-week course on the island of Ibiza run by none other than Lama Yeshe.

"I'd never seen anyone like him," said Maria. "His energy, the power coming out of him, was incredible. He was transmitting with his face, his hands, his whole body—every way he could to make us understand."

Later, the Hita Torreses, together with their French friend François Camus, discussed the idea of starting a retreat center in Spain. After Lama Yeshe gave his blessing to the idea, for six years Paco and François put all their energy and money into building not only a meditation house and retreat cabins, but also a road leading up to them, on a remote block of land in the Alpujarra mountains.

With the benefit of hindsight, one highly auspicious event preceded Ösel's birth. The Dalai Lama made a sudden, unscheduled visit to the retreat center, which he named Ösel-Ling or "Place of Clear Light," referring to the clear light of the most subtle mind which is the goal of meditators. Given His Holiness' hectic schedule, it seemed an unusual detour to such a remote and insignificant outpost.

It also seems ironic, in retrospect, that Maria had once complained to Lama Yeshe about how her children prevented her from going on retreats. His reply? "Your children are your retreat. You should relate to each one of them as though they are a Buddha, because you never know who they are."

Early signs

From the very start, there was something markedly different about Ösel Hita Torres. His birth had been incredibly easy—just one contraction, with no pain to his mother, and he emerged into the world, eyes open and serene. He slept through every night from the day he was born, never crying, even when hungry. He was self-contained, not needing to be with the other children. And he had the most unusual concentration for a baby, holding and looking at subtle things, like a single hair, for long periods. Around the time of his arrival, the family's fortunes also swiftly changed, with Paco finding lots of new building work.

Maria and Paco had, of course, discussed the idea that their baby might be the reincarnation of Lama Yeshe, but the idea was something of an irrelevant fantasy given their busy lives raising a family of five and trying to help manage a retreat center.

The first clear signal that Ösel might have a very special future ahead of him came when they took him, as a baby, to a ceremony at an FPMT center in Germany. Lama Zopa, Lama Yeshe's former student and now head of FPMT, noticed the baby and asked his name. Later, during the ceremony, he said, "Lama is very close to us at this moment. He might even be in the room with us."

Two months later, Lama Zopa visited Ösel-Ling to give a course. During a tea break, Maria left the meditation room and came back to find that Lama Zopa had lifted Ösel to the teaching throne with him. Later the lama questioned Maria in detail about aspects of the baby's birth. Although he didn't say anything explicitly, when he left he gave Maria Lama Yeshe's mala, a set of rosary beads used to count mantras.

The possible link between Lama Yeshe and Ösel, while intriguing, was once again pushed into the background of the Hita Torres' busy domestic lives. Unbeknownst to Maria and Paco, however, Lama Zopa had been trying to track down the reincarnation of Lama Yeshe for some time. Several clairvoyant advisors had given precise indications suggesting that Ösel was he—back in India the names Maria and Paco, and Ösel's place of birth, had all been mentioned by different oracles. Nonetheless, in accordance with the precise procedures set down for identifying tulkus—lamas who have voluntarily been reborn to help others become enlightened—Lama Zopa investigated a number of possible options before, in April 1986, asking Maria to bring Ösel with him to Delhi to meet the Dalai Lama.

An auspicious first meeting was followed by a lengthy journey to Dharamsala, and subsequent tests. These included presenting Ösel with ritual objects that had been favorites of Lama Yeshe's, alongside nearly identical, as well as more attractive, alternatives. In each case, Ösel correctly selected "his" own object. Formally recognized as the legitimate incarnation of Lama Yeshe, Ösel began formal training in the new Sera monastery in India in preparation for his new life as a Westerner teaching the Dharma.

Nearly two decades later, he has received both a traditional monastic education, as well as a Western one, his curriculum sensitively guided by Lama Zopa. Given the rigor of the Tibetan Buddhist system, he is still to undergo a further ten to fifteen years of study before he begins his own teaching practice. But already he has demonstrated the same energy, strength of purpose, and commitment to helping others as he did in his pre-vious lifetime. He has also confirmed his former identity in myriad ways. These are described in Mackenzie's compelling book *Reincarnation: The Boy Lama*, which provides many fasci-nating insights into the Lama Yeshe/Lama Ösel story and from which I have drawn much of this material.

Who are our children?

I have chosen Lama Ösel to illustrate how highly realized beings can master the death process mainly because the work of both Lama Yeshe and Lama Zopa is well-advanced in the West, and FPMT is a global organization.

But there is nothing unique about this particular case. The more you seek, the more examples you find of reincarnated tulkus born in America, Canada, New Zealand, and other Western countries. Several intriguing examples are given in another of Mackenzie's books, *Reborn in the West*. In some cases, such as that of Jetsunma, who now runs a center just out-side Washington, DC, children have been born and brought up in homes with a variety of religions, but conducted Bud-dhist practices, without knowing what they were, until "coin-cidences" later in life revealed not only their Buddhist path, but their former identity.

Mention should also be made of the growing evidence emerging in the area of past-life regression, where individuals in a deeply relaxed or hypnotized state are able vividly to recall incidents which they appear to have experienced in previous lives. While not a Buddhist practice, this supports the concept of rebirth taken for granted not only in the East but also among more orthodox Jewish groups and by the early

Christian church until it was banned by the Emperor Justinian I in A.D. 543.

While Buddhist teachings about this precious life focus on the need to fulfill our true potential, the concept of birth and rebirth, so new to our Western way of thinking, presents us with mind-boggling possibilities. Who were my partner, my children, my friends, my pets in a previous lifetime, and what karma brought us together? Who was I? Could karma and rebirth explain why it is we find ourselves so powerfully drawn to some people—and repelled by others?

Similarly, in thinking about our future, instead of concentrating on the next few years, or at most, on our retirement, what about abandoning our "Mickey Mouse minds," our sesame seed-size preoccupations, and taking in the big picture? What about our fifty-year plan? Our next lifetime plan? Here, surely, is a goal worthy of our energy, purpose, and extraordinary good fortune.

6. The First Step

TAKING REFUGE

Vision is not enough. It must be combined with venture. It is not enough to stare up the steps, we must also step up the stairs.

———————————— VACLAV HAVEL ————————————

I T WAS THIS PARTICULAR lifetime, rather than a more panoramic vision, that was preoccupying me after Janmarie and I left London. New York was our first stop in a round-the-world journey which would take us to a number of stops in the USA before traveling on to Fiji and then the Great Barrier Reef.

I have always been drawn to the United States. I marvel at how from such unique and diverse backgrounds—from the quaint charm of New England villages to the *nouveau riche* vulgarity of Las Vegas, from the sultry torpor of the Deep South to the vast industrialism of the North—the American people appear united in their patriotism and confidence. It is an example from which other divided, self-loathing countries could learn.

While my wife wanted to experience Broadway and Times Square for the first time, I had visited the Big Apple before and hadn't much enjoyed the experience. Sure, New York's scale and energy was truly impressive, but there was also a sullen, self-absorbed incivility about the place which I hadn't warmed to. Later I was to discover this was as much a mask as the apparent unfriendliness of Londoners.

This particular visit was both brief and dominated by news from London. My literary agent had sent out sample chapters and a summary of my proposed novel *Conflict of Interest*, soon after the publication of *The Invisible Persuaders*, to several UK publishers. And much to my surprise and delight, not just one but two wanted to buy it. The first offer was a derisory sum, but as soon as the second publisher entered the fray, that offer was doubled and after further haggling, doubled again. Faxes would be brought up to our hotel room with the latest offers from London. A one-book deal became a two-book deal within a matter of hours. Lengthy marketing proposals hummed through the fax machine, promising to turn me into a major international bestselling novelist—a phrase I will never forget for its breathtaking audacity.

Thrilled though I was by this latest turn of events, there was also something disturbing about what was happening. How was it possible that something which had been worth £25,000 one day was worth £50,000 a couple of days later? The words on the page hadn't changed. Nothing about the story was different. But the publisher's intentions had clearly shifted. It was a consideration I tried to push to the back of my mind, but which remained in my thoughts for a long while afterwards.

In the meantime, the flurry of activity continued until, in a dizzying finale, the auction came to an end. I accepted an offer representing the equivalent of about eighteen months' income—long enough, I hoped, to write both the novels for which I was now contracted. Best of all was the assurance of my publishers-to-be that they took a long-term view of my writing career. Their intention was to build me up as a brand, book by book, until I achieved bestsellerdom.

Having secured a deal in London, my agent assured me, in a bullish mood, that New York was next on the list, to be followed by Hollywood. Foreign rights were also talked up. Translations into a multitude of foreign languages seemed in the offing. In a celebratory mood, Janmarie and I dined out at The Plaza, a favored haunt of my all-time favorite author, F. Scott Fitzgerald. As we quaffed champagne in the Oak Room on a night at the top, my writing career, so long frustrated, had never seemed so bright with promise.

It would be tempting to attach undue karmic significance to what, in retrospect, turned out to be several years of incredibly good fortune. I had moved out of a stressful job into a far more rewarding lifestyle, which had been followed by publication deals that had so far eluded me. Was this something to do with my starting to meditate, I wondered, or my first halting steps on the dharma path? Perhaps. But the reality is that I know many Buddhists whose practice has been incomparably greater than mine, but who have suffered devastating material reversals. Short-term karmic prizes are always possible, but conditioning the mind is a life-long process.

What this new development did provide was freedom of choice in where we might live next. Having been born and raised in Rhodesia—as Zimbabwe was known in colonial times—and spent my early adult life in South Africa, I had left my heart in that continent. Its compelling power over those who feel they belong there has been described by far better writers than me, among them Elspeth Huxley, who in

White Man's Country (1935) describes how Africa's invisible hold endures:

> . . . in the memory of those who have left it, flashing back on to the mind so vividly that the nostrils seem to sense the sweet smell of a vlei after the rains or the tingling of red dust from untarred roads, the ear to catch the melancholy hoot of a rain-bird or the strangely moving rhythmic chant from the throats of distant Africans.

Deeply as I wished to return, however, I had to think with my head, not my heart; I could see no long-term future for a white professional in southern Africa.

In seeking a better quality of life, with sunshine, space, and a less frenetic lifestyle, we eventually decided on Perth, Western Australia. It was Janmarie's hometown and soon became my own. Perched on the edge of the Indian Ocean, it is one of the most isolated cities in the world, which is perhaps why it provides such a wonderful quality of life, including endless white sand beaches, a Mediterranean climate, and a modern city center noticeably free of grime, graffiti, or any other form of rubbish. A few hours south are the vineyards of Margaret River, and further on still the mountain forests and rugged coastline of Denmark and Albany. Once settled, I began work on Conflict of Interest.

One of the first things that became apparent, after a period in transition, was how much time we suddenly had. Instead of traveling forty-five minutes to an hour each way to work, or to see clients, commute time was now more like ten minutes. Free of the stresses of life in a big city, suddenly we had whole evenings to ourselves. Had I not received any teachings on leisure and fortune I would still have felt lucky; it was as if the lid had been taken off the pressure-cooker I had been living in since moving to London, and now we had time to breathe. But after Rinpoche's teachings I was even more mindful of the extreme rarity of my good fortune. Making some inquiries about Tibetan Buddhist classes in Perth, I decided I could do worse than visit the organization closest to where I lived—the Tibetan Buddhist Society (TBS).

I had continued my morning meditating since London, but missing was a sense of direction. My concentration was improving, slowly, but where was all this heading? Little did I know that in making my way to TBS I couldn't have chosen a better place to move things forward to the next stage.

There was real vibrancy in TBS's Mount Lawley gompa when I made my first visit. I can vividly remember thinking how very different this was from Glebe Street—the thangkas and statues were much the same, but the energy in the room was altogether more upbeat. Was this Aussie exuberance in action, I wondered? Or was it a lifestyle thing? You would certainly never have seen shorts and T-shirts in Glebe Street— most of the year it would have been far too cold.

The true cause of the buzz, as I soon discovered, was the teacher, Les Sheehy. A true-blue Aussie, born and raised in Perth, Les is also a very busy person. As well as running several businesses, being a husband and father, and providing community services such as stress management courses and counseling, he also teaches at least two evenings a week, leads meditation retreats several times a year, and with his wife Marg manages most aspects of TBS's administration. Dynamic, direct, and a powerful communicator, Les is well known for his straight down the line approach to the Dharma—and, like most Buddhist teachers, a completely irreverent sense of humor.

"Today we're at the chapter on Taking Refuge," he began, taking out Geshe Loden's *Path to Enlightenment* which, weighing in at over 1.2 kilograms and more than 6 centimeters thick, is probably the most comprehensive Lam Rim commentary in English. "So I'd like to start with a question."

There were mock groans from around the gompa.

"A simple one," he grinned. "A definition, please. What is a Buddhist?"

There wasn't much of a pause before someone volunteered, "A person who follows Buddha's teachings?"

"Which ones?" demanded Les. "It's said that Buddha gave eighty-four thousand teachings. How many would you have to follow to get in the gate?"

"Someone who wants to become enlightened?" offered another student.

Les shook his head. "Vipassana Buddhists, the Southern School, don't aspire to enlightenment. They aspire to nirvana, which is different. But you can't say they're not Buddhists."

After a pause, a student at the front offered, "Someone who takes refuge in the three jewels."

"Thank you, Richard," said Les, before looking round the room. "Did everyone get that? A Buddhist is someone who takes refuge in the Buddha, the Dharma, and the Sangha."

Then, as all heads were nodding in recognition: "Another question. What are the reasons for taking refuge?"

"It depends on your motivation," someone suggested.

"Very good," Les was nodding. "You'll remember how important intention is in determining karma? It's also extremely important to understand what is motivating you to follow the Dharma."

Why we follow the path

A young monk asked the Master, "How can I ever get emancipated?"
The Master replied, "Who has ever put you in bondage?"

ADVAITA LESSON

Buddha gave numerous teachings to people with a diverse range of intelligence, understanding and motivation, explained Les. In simple terms, he talked to people in language they could understand. To return to the analogy of the lotus rooted in the bed of the swamp and flowering on the surface, we are all at different stages of growth.

The most basic level of motivation, from a Buddhist perspective, arises from the recognition of several factors: what if our mindstream *does* have an existence after this lifetime? What if causes *do* create effects according to the law of karma? Just as a sensible person plans his life beyond his day-to-day needs, shouldn't we look beyond the immediate horizons of this particular lifetime?

This level of motivation is a good starting point. It helps us get the ups and downs of our life into better perspective. When we think about the bigger picture, our inevitable frustrations and despair become somehow more manageable.

But that's not where things end. A deeper analysis of life, as encapsulated in Buddha's Four Noble Truths, shows that if we want to experience true happiness, we should be striving for a future outside samsara.

Samsara is often used as shorthand for cyclic existence, the endless round of birth, aging, sickness, and death which we have all experienced since beginningless time. But a truer definition of samsara is "mind afflicted by karma and delusion." It is this mind which perpetuates our experience of cyclic existence; its opposite, a mind free from karma and delusion, is defined as nirvana.

It is highly significant that neither samsara nor nirvana depend on our being in a particular physical place or state. Nirvana isn't a Buddhist version of heaven, which we must die to experience. Nor does samsara end with death. Best of all, each one of us has the opportunity to achieve nirvana in this very lifetime.

Because Buddhism is a living tradition, we can find examples of people who have achieved nirvana. They may go through exactly the same things as we do, but instead of responding with, for example, envy or impatience, their mental state is one of unchanging peace and happiness. Look at the Dalai Lama as an example of the end result of Buddhist practices. As a leader who has lost his country, a sensitive man who has seen many of his friends killed and tortured, it would be understandable if he had become an immensely bitter and vengeful individual. But most people who have had the privilege of meeting him will confirm that he positively radiates bliss and serenity. In fact, it is impossible to imagine anyone happier!

Renunciation

Many Buddhists take the view that they've experienced enough karma and delusions to last all their many lifetimes, and aspire to break free from samsara altogether. In the words of the Dalai Lama, "When the thought that aspires to transcend the world arises within you as strongly as the thought of finding an exit would arise in a person caught in a burning house, you have become a spiritual aspirant of intermediate perspective."

This motivation is also known as renunciation, a word which can conjure up unattractive images of self-denial, but which in this sense means simply "turning away from the causes of dissatisfaction." The recognition that worldly attainments just do not provide enduring happiness, and that we need to work on the internals, rather than the externals, is an important motivation. It is also the basis of achieving nirvana, often represented by the lotus flower. It is no accident that most statues of Buddha have him sitting on cushions resting on a lotus flower—the symbol of renunciation.

But what if we achieve nirvana? What if, through extreme diligence, we attain its supreme peace and happiness? Would that be enough, or is there a more profound level of motivation still?

Some years ago a number of tourists were kidnapped by terrorists in the Philippines, and held hostage in the jungle for many months. Finally they were released in small groups. I will never forget the reaction of one hostage who was interviewed at the airport on his way home to join his wife, who had been freed just days earlier.

You would think that after months of extreme privation and the constant threat of uncertainty and death, returning safely to one's wife, home, and family would be a cause for joyful celebration. But the hostage, while relieved, could only think of the group of hostages he'd left behind. Those who, in the preceding months, had been his fellow prisoners, whom he now knew better than anyone else, and with whom in several cases, he had formed unique and profound bonds of attachment. His overriding concern was to ensure that those still being held captive would be safely released to experience the same freedom he had now. Only then would he really be able to celebrate.

Bodhichitta

In the same way, Buddhist practitioners with the deepest motivation aspire not only to break free of samsara themselves, but to help all other sentient beings achieve the same freedom. This motivation is known in Buddhism as "bodhichitta," which we can approximately translate here as "compassion," and more than any other concept is what defines the Tibetan Buddhist, who aspires to attain personal enlightenment in order to help all others become enlightened too. As a Buddha, not only will we experience limitless bliss ourselves, we will also be best able to lead all other sentient beings from the sufferings of samsara.

This may seem a very grand and noble purpose—because it is! It is the ultimate motivation that can be conceived. Which is why Buddhism might be regarded as an extremely optimistic tradition—we set our sights on the absolute highest peak of accomplishment, and then proceed towards it, step-by-step, supported in our efforts by the example of all Buddhas, past and present, the teachings of Shakyamuni Buddha two and a half thousand years ago, and our fellow travelers on the path.

Given the importance of bodhichitta, which like most dharma subjects is profound, the whole of the next chapter is devoted to it. In symbolic terms, just as renunciation is represented by a lotus, bodhichitta is symbolized by a silver-colored moon cushion, on which Buddha is usually represented sitting.

In the introduction to this book I said that Lam Rim approximately translates as the "Path to Enlightenment." More accurately it is the "Graduated Path to Enlightenment"—with the deepening levels of motivation defining the graduations.

In our enthusiasm to embrace the Dharma, it's important that we allow our own motivation to unfold in a sincere and heartfelt way, rather than try to save all sentient beings on day one. Renunciation, for example, is an especially tricky motivation. In theory we may buy into the idea. While reading dharma books, or listening to teachings, we may accept it absolutely. But then we go about our normal lives, and habitual patterns of behavior reassert themselves, and we continue creating causes which we know can only bring negative results. Yes, we want to achieve enlightenment, we may think, but can't we have the nice bits of samsara too?!

Buddhism offers a wealth of antidotes to use when we catch ourselves out like this. In many ways the Lam Rim might be regarded as a manual, packed with practices to oppose dissatisfaction, a toolbox of concepts and techniques designed for every occasion.

It is also as well to remember that we're on a journey of transformation which will take not only the rest of this lifetime, but maybe lifetimes to come. Like the flabby businessman arriving at the gym for a fitness appraisal, we should not expect to emerge trim, taut, and terrific after a couple of weeks on the circuit. Patient application of discipline and energy will be required. We should be confident of achieving success if we persist—there are plenty of role models around us.

But the important thing is to take that first step.

Taking refuge: What it is and what it is not

The only true failure lies in failure to start.

HAROLD BLAKE WALKER

Taking refuge is usually defined as establishing a safe or a clear direction. When we take refuge we are self-consciously committing ourselves to the Buddha, as an example of the enlightenment we wish to achieve, the Dharma, his teachings, as the most effective way to attain enlightenment, and the Sangha, or community of Buddhists, as a means of encouragement and support on our journey. These are often referred to as "the three jewels" or "triple gem."

Participating in a "Taking Refuge" ceremony with one's teacher is often regarded as the point at which one officially becomes a Buddhist. The ceremony can last as little as ten minutes and in Tibetan Buddhism requires one to repeat a verse along the following lines:

> In the Buddha, the Dharma and the Sangha
> I take refuge until becoming enlightened;
> By the practice of giving and so on,
> May I attain Buddhahood to benefit all beings.

While this is a serious commitment for the individual concerned, taking refuge is not a social occasion, like a baptism or bar mitzvah, and the event itself, while significant, is not considered to have dramatically changed one's future. Personal transformation is an evolutionary process.

Having taken refuge for the first time, Buddhists are generally required to repeat the above verse at least three times a day, as a reminder of the objectives we are pursuing. Thereafter, in the words of the Dalai Lama, "Being mindful of all activities of body, speech, and mind, we should continue our life with our practice kept as an inner treasure, not as an ornament to be flaunted before others. There is a Tibetan saying: 'Change your mind; leave the rest as it is.' This is particularly good advice for beginners."

In the West, where our natural impulse is to express things in material terms, you sometimes find enthusiasts wearing dresses or robes which imitate those of ordained nuns and monks, mala beads wrapped around their wrists, or sporting shaven heads. You may hear such people trumpeting their vegetarianism, claiming transcendent levels of bliss, or adopting mannerisms that imply great saintliness or higher powers.

All traditions have their embarrassing adherents, and Buddhism is no exception. In true Tibetan Buddhism, the most highly realized practitioners are at pains to emphasize their ordinariness. The Dalai Lama insists he is "a simple monk" and most Buddhists take their cue from this. There is an amusing report about a very high-ranking lama who, arriving in America to open a dharma center, began his first evening by stressing that, far from being the astral-traveling wunderkind his audience had perhaps been hoping for, he was just a regular monk with no realizations. Disappointed by this revelation, in a culture where spectacular overclaim is regarded as the norm, very few people turned up to his second evening and the center didn't get off the ground.

It is also the case that taking refuge, and the process of renunciation, doesn't involve donating all our hard-earned savings to charity, throwing in our jobs, and looking for a position in the local soup kitchen. To make an instant change to one's material circumstances would be to miss the point. Besides, the old cliché is not "money is the root of all evil" but "love of money is the root of all evil." One legend I particularly like which illustrates this involves a Buddhist monk who visited a wealthy prince. Traditionally, monks are allowed very few possessions— two changes of clothes and a begging bowl in which to collect food. Since it was a hot day, the prince suggested they go out into the garden of his opulent estate. There they were, quite some distance from the prince's home, when a servant came racing towards them. "There's a fire at the palace! The whole building is burning down!"

The reaction of the monk was to leap to his feet. "My bowl! I left it in the palace!" he cried, as he headed off to try to salvage it. The prince, on the other hand, was dismissive: all that was being destroyed were material things to which he felt little attachment. What you own, in short, is of far less consequence than the nature of your attitude towards it.

Taking refuge, like most other Buddhist practices, is about rearranging the internals, not the externals. It is not about giving the appearance of being a Buddhist, or pronouncing your belief in Buddhism. Nor is it about dramatically altering your financial circumstances. What really matters, as the Dalai Lama says, is being mindful of actions of body, speech, and mind, and making sure they are consistent with the objectives we set ourselves in taking refuge.

I have often reflected that, in our interactions with others, if one was to videotape for a day a Buddhist behaving in accordance with dharma teachings, a Christian acting consistently with the Scriptures, and a Muslim observing the Koran, at the end of that day an objective viewer wouldn't be able to tell one adherent from another.

In short, we may feel inspired and enormously privileged to have the opportunity to work towards the enlightenment of all sentient beings, but there's no need to draw attention to ourselves. Taking refuge is important, but it's only the first step in a journey of transformation. It's our membership card to the gym. The real work lies ahead.

7. Cultivating Compassion

THE HEART OF ENLIGHTENMENT

All the joy the world contains
Comes through wishing happiness for others.
All the misery the world contains
Comes through wanting pleasure for oneself.

———— SHANTIDEVA, *Engaging in the Bodhisattva Deeds* ————

IMAGINE THIS SCENE: YOU have been found guilty of some unknown but terrible crime, and are about to be sentenced. There is no question of being let off lightly. A fine would be too lenient. So would a jail term. In the surreal state in which you find yourself, the judge has created a cruel, round-the-clock punishment especially for you.

You are to be taken from the courthouse and returned to your everyday life, giving the appearance that you've been set free. The catch is, you are to be accompanied everywhere you go by an invisible being. This being is just like you in every respect—not so bad, you might think at first. Where the punishment comes in is that your unseen companion never stops talking. You soon discover that from the moment you wake up in the morning—even before you've opened your eyes—to the moment you finally fall asleep, you're being talked at. Yada, yada, yada. Blah, blah, blah. There's no escaping the punishment—you don't even get five minutes' peace and quiet in the bathroom—the judge has explicitly ordered that you are *never* to be left alone.

Most of the time your unseen torturer rambles on in a chaotic stream of consciousness. He has some lucid moments. But even these drive you crazy, because the invisible being only ever talks about one subject and one subject alone: me, myself, I—24/7! Want more, now! Gimme, gimme, gimme!

No one else is aware of the endless chatter of, let's call him, Self. Which is just as well. If Self's constant monologue were to be broadcast on radio, you would soon be shunned, not only on account of Self's frequent, unsavory preoccupations— which nice people like you and your friends wouldn't want to be associated with—but also because he is so completely me-focused.

This story is, sadly, far less fictitious than we mostly care to admit. Self seems ever-present, if not in our faces, then insistently whispering at us from in the wings. But when we try to turn the spotlight on him, to pin him down, to make him accountable for some disastrous episode, like McCavity in T.S. Eliot's *Cats* he's never there.

The wiliest of operators, the very ultimate in spin-doctors when he needs to be, Self makes sure that when we do see him, he is the master of the plausible explanation. It is not Self's vanity or egotism that caused you to lose your temper with someone—no way, that person was being outrageously provocative. It is not Self's constant need for self-aggrandizement or material props that has you pushing your credit limit—on the contrary, you're just trying to give your family a better quality of life!

Even when we do succeed in seeing through Self's brilliantly devious spin, and recognize what a dangerous influence he is, for the most part we're so used to him and his endless carping that we've come to think of it as normal. Natural. Intrinsic to who we are.

More than that, let anyone else so much as hint that they've caught a glimpse of Self and don't much like what they see, far from agreeing with them about this unhappy state of affairs, we'll feel hurt or angry and leap to Self's defense. Like kidnapping victims suffering from Stockholm Syndrome (who start to empathize, then fall in love, with their captors), even though we know that Self is ranting, negative, and obsessive, the bizarre truth is that we love him more than anything, and are at pains to indulge his every whim. We do our best to make him feel special, brilliant, successful, popular, wealthy, powerful, enlightened, or whatever trip he happens to be on. Most frightening of all, somewhere along the way we allow Self to so dominate our consciousness that we even start to think of him as our essence. Our true being. Our "real me."

Popular magazines lecture to us that allowing Self expression is one of the highest goals of human beings. When other people thwart this, they are jeopardizing our chances of happiness, and we should break free from such negative people and situations. Motivators tell us to believe in ourselves. How's that for a giveaway? We're not ever asked to believe in a Mercedes-Benz car, or gravity, or a Mozart concerto, so why the need to believe in Self? The fact is, Self has a very dark and painful secret, and depends on our belief for his survival a lot more than we generally realize. Of which more later.

Society sets great store in protecting the rights of Self. Advertisers play directly to Self's monomania. And the desire to give Self his fifteen minutes of fame, to make him feel important, is constantly being exploited in new and creative ways.

From a Buddhist point of view, the veneration of Self is just plain crazy; we couldn't be more effectively guaranteeing our own misery if we tried. For all our dissatisfaction, every last ache of suffering we experience can be traced back to our habitual indulging of Self.

This observation is by no means unique to Buddhism. There is a growing trend among contemporary psychologists to consider the cult of Self to have gone too far. And no doubt one of the reasons the Dharma is becoming so popular in the West is that so many of us are waking up to the recognition that it directly addresses the prevailing unhappiness of our time.

Some statistics: in Western nations, about 60 percent of households used to include children, now only 12 percent do. More than 80 percent of our elderly live alone or with a spouse rather than as part of a family household, compared with 25 percent a century ago. Divorce, almost unheard of in the 1950s, now ends at least one out of three marriages, with major knock-on consequences for children growing up in one-parent families. By 2021 more than 40 percent of men and one-third of women will be living on their own.

By that same time, according to the World Health Organization, depression will be the second most common cause of death after heart disease. Depression, anxiety, and other mental conditions afflict an increasingly large proportion of the population. Antidepressants alone are the third largest therapy class of all pharmaceutical sales, with over $13 billion sold each year, and a growth rate of 18 percent (IMS Health Data 2000 World Review).

How do we account for these seismic shifts in the way we live? Is it that we've all developed such bizarre fundamental incompatibilities with each other that relationships have far less chance of survival? Have human beings in the West become so pharmacologically imbalanced that we need to ingest billions of dollars worth of drugs to get us back to normal?

It's an amazing paradox: the more we focus on making ourselves happy, the unhappier we become. We remain convinced that attracting money, love, and influence to ourselves is the road to happiness. Conventional consumerism and social beliefs support this delusion. But an honest assessment of the facts—whether the microcosm of our individual loneliness, or the macro trend of antidepressant consumption—reveals the same incontrovertible evidence that me-ism makes us miserable. Or in the words of Shantideva:

> We all seek happiness, but turn our backs on it.
> We all wish to avoid misery, but race to collect
> its causes.

Writing in the *New Internationalist* magazine, psychiatrist and writer Trevor Turner said, "Today a rising tide of narcissism is spreading like toxic social algae . . . Conditions such as air rage, road rage, and dysmorphophobia (the conviction that you don't quite look right) all reflect the triumph of individual desire over a commitment to the world outside oneself."

The Buddhist response to the paradox of narcissism is both simple and profound: altruism is the cause of the abiding happiness we all seek.

While many of us may agree this is a pleasant-sounding theory, putting it into practice is a different matter entirely. As the Dalai Lama says, "Ignorance and the I-grasping syndrome have been with us since beginningless time, and the instincts of attachment, aversion, anger, jealousy, and so forth are very deeply rooted in our mindstreams. Eliminating them is not as simple as turning on a light to chase away the darkness of a room."

Fortunately, Buddhism provides us with creative, radical, and powerful tools to help us on what will probably be a lifetime's mission. Just as the law of cause and effect shows us that it's in our own selfish interests to be generous, so too our understanding of bodhichitta can profoundly alter our attitudes to others.

Being wisely selfish

Make it a practice when something is done, no matter by whom,
to ask yourself, "What is their intention in doing this?"
But start with yourself; examine yourself first.

MARCUS AURELIUS

What exactly is meant by the word "bodhichitta" (pronounced *body-cheetah*)? A strict definition is "the desire to achieve enlightenment for the sake of others." While technically correct, those ten words only begin to convey the underlying motivation of bodhichitta, which is one of profound compassion for all living beings. The Dalai Lama often describes Buddhism in simple terms as "loving-kindness." He is referring here to bodhichitta, which is both a part of the Path to Enlightenment and at the same time its all-encompassing purpose.

It was when Buddha experienced the suffering that sickness, old age, and death inflicted on those around him that he decided to change his self-centered lifestyle. With this came the recognition that staying behind the palace gates, not having to think of anyone but himself, was not bringing him the happiness he wanted.

For most of us, walking away from our worldly lives to become a monk or nun is not an appealing option. But nor do we need to. We can, instead, work towards a metaphorical departure, by replacing the tendency of Self to dominate our thoughts with deliberate practices to include thoughts of others.

As busy people it's easy to think that we just don't have the time to think about others any more than we already do. "I'm stressed out enough trying to manage my own responsibilities and those of my family," you may reason. "If I start taking chunks of time out of my schedule, no matter how noble the cause, I just won't stay on top of things."

But the issue is not so much one of time as of attitude. Two partners in a law firm may both receive demanding emails at 5:20 P.M. requiring them to work late—for the third night in a row. One may think, "This *@*#!! client! He's wrecking my personal life! Who the hell does that *@*#!! think he is anyway?! The shoe will be on the other foot when I slug him with my fees. In fact, I'll add an extra five hours just for the inconvenience." The other partner may think, "Well, here's a great opportunity to practice patience. By working to give my client exactly what he wants, may I be creating the direct cause for myself, and all living beings, to achieve enlightenment quickly and easily."

The second partner isn't necessarily a saint—or crazy. There may very well be an ironic tone to this thought as it passes through his mind. But the simple act of thinking it, of attributing some higher purpose to his work, helps take the steam out. Both partners have to stay on late—they have no choice about that. But they *can* choose what attitude they adopt, and bodhichitta motivation is far more conducive to countering stress than the "poor me" victim mentality which we slip into so very easily.

There's another important benefit. One of the biggest problems of busy people is that we feel so much of what we do is ultimately pointless. Both partners probably recognize the relative unimportance of the work for which they have to stay late. Sure, the client may be kicking and screaming right now, but in six weeks' time the whole thing will have been forgotten, overtaken by other events with their own, short-lived urgency. What's more, there's nothing special about the task in hand—any one of hundreds of lawyers could do just as good a job. How is someone to get any special sense of fulfillment out of all that?

With bodhichitta motivation, *everything* we do matters. There is nothing more selfless than wishing to help others, and there is no higher goal than enlightenment. By reminding ourselves of our purpose to help all others reach this state, we imbue enormous positive energy to whatever we do. Which is why one partner may leave the office at 10:00 P.M., angry at having been robbed of an evening, while the other may head home at the same time far less stressed, in the knowledge that his sacrifice hasn't been wasted. If this were just a once only event, the difference in their mental states may not matter. But over the course of months or even years, we should have no trouble recognizing that one of these lawyers is likelier to enjoy a far better quality of life than the other. This may eventually translate into a healthier physical state, with lower stress levels and blood pressure, and higher resistance to disease.

This second attitude is one the Dalai Lama refers to as "being wisely selfish." We want to be happy, so the best thing we can do is to contribute to the happiness of others. This shift in thinking doesn't come easily, nor overnight. But the Dharma provides us with a number of arguments to help us accept bodhichitta, both in our minds and in our hearts. Let's look at these before seeing how to put bodhichitta into action.

Recognizing the benefits of bodhichitta

The first argument is to weigh up the benefits of bodhichitta. The problem most people have when they encounter bodhichitta is that it sounds altogether idealistic. It's all very well spending your life thinking about others, they feel, but all that'll happen is you'll be used as a doormat. People will exploit your good nature. You'll end up chewed up and spat out—and how's that supposed to help anybody?

As I hope is already clear, Buddhism does not encourage weakness, and its purpose is to empower, not to create victims. If anything, the frequently heard expression "look out for number one" is a testament to the deceptive and debilitating narcissism which is the true cause of so much unhappiness.

If we look around with an open mind, do we find that thinking of others is a source of happiness, or is it really more effective to focus on looking after yourself?

Two senior sisters in my neighborhood provide a useful case study. Both have been widows for some years and the Meals on Wheels service plays an important part in each of their lives. For Phyllis, the 75-year-old, money plays no part in her reliance on the charity to provide meals three times a week. Instead, it's convenient not to have to cook a main meal every day, and she likes seeing the people who bring her food. Being of advanced years, she doesn't get out very much, and as a result suffers from loneliness and depression. The value of Meals on Wheels lies not only in the food, but also in positive interaction it provides in Phyllis' ever-shrinking world.

By contrast, her older sister Daphne wasn't left very well provided for, and the three meals she gets every week from Meals on Wheels make a real difference to her modest weekly budget. Despite her financial situation, however, Daphne is a bright-eyed, sprightly woman with a busy schedule and strong sense of purpose. Far from closing in, her world continues to keep her busy and stimulated, mostly because of her voluntary work for Meals on Wheels. She is one of the ladies who delivers food to homes in several suburbs—including her sister's. She knows a lot of people, including "all the oldies" as she describes her clients, as well as the Meals on Wheels team at HQ. She keeps abreast of developments on the staff notice board. She's invited to summer lunches and Christmas parties. Daphne may be older and poorer than Phyllis, but you wouldn't have to spend more than two minutes in the company of each sister to decide who was happier.

Including others in our thoughts contributes to our happiness. Thinking only of ourselves makes us miserable. Examples like that of Phyllis and Daphne show us this, but even more powerful is our own experience. If we look back through our own lives to the time we were at our unhappiest, it's interesting to recollect what we were thinking of. Or rather, who.

I can remember, very clearly, one of the lowest points in my life. Living on my own in London, the only girl I was interested in had a helicopter-owning boyfriend with whom I couldn't possibly compete. My career was becalmed by the recession of the early 1990s. As for my writing ambitions, I felt I had wasted my entire adult life chasing an illusion.

The common element in all these depression-causing thoughts was, of course, "me." Drinking more than I should, and taking tranquilizers to block the pain, it seemed to me that the only way I could ever be happy was if the helicopter-flying boyfriend plunged into the icy North Atlantic, a fantastic job offer landed in my lap, or my true genius was recognized by a publisher! Until that time, the best I could do was to anesthetize myself from reality.

I sometimes wonder what my reaction would have been if I'd been told that my unhappiness was self-inflicted. However tactfully worded, I don't think I would have taken the suggestion seriously (or kindly). Even though I might have recognized that the way I interpreted reality was part of the problem, but how exactly was I to change it?

As it happened, circumstances did change, and my life moved on, though I discovered that the things I thought I wanted came with their own built-in challenges. Only later was I able to see things in some kind of perspective.

It is true we can think of some circumstances where unhappiness doesn't stem from self-obsession. The profound concern of a parent for a child diagnosed with a terrible disease is one example. But this doesn't in any way negate bodhichitta. Among the parents who best survive such a harrowing ordeal are those who recognize their child's problem as part of a much bigger picture. They may get involved in, or start, support groups and charities. They use their own tragedy as a catalyst to help others. Instead of allowing themselves to feel like the victims of a cruel god or indifferent universe, they move on from the past with something positive.

Each of us needs to perform our own analysis, looking at the lives of those around us as well as our own. With unflinching honesty we need to revisit our own darkest hours and ask ourselves, How much of my unhappiness came from thinking too much of myself? Would I have benefited by engaging more positively with others?

Conversely, what about the times I have experienced deep, heartfelt happiness? What were my preoccupations then, and can I recreate them?

Recognizing that we have the freedom to choose what and who we think about may not seem a major revelation. But within this simple truth lies the source of both immeasurable happiness—and sorrow.

Self vs. Other

Another argument in favor of bodhichitta is that of equanimity. We all have an inherent tendency to classify those around us into "friends," "enemies," and "strangers." This categorization subsequently dictates our attitudes and behavior. Oscar Wilde once mischievously declared that "morality is the attitude we adopt to those whom we personally dislike." We might turn a blind eye to our friends' shortcomings, but we show no such tolerance when other people behave the same way.

Buddhism challenges this innate but illogical tendency. We only need to stop and think for two minutes to see that the person we now hold dearest to us was once a total stranger, and that we can no longer bear the sight of some people whose company we used to relish. The categories of "friend," "enemy" and "stranger" are therefore not fixed, but liable to change at short notice, often when we least expect them to.

I particularly like the story of Charlotte Van Beuningen, the

Dutch wartime heroine. After Germany invaded Holland, she lost touch with her son—who had been in the army—and her daughters. As if this wasn't bad enough, she found herself with a houseful of billeted German soldiers.

In February 1942, a large concentration camp was set up near her home in Rotterdam to imprison anyone accused of resistance. News soon came through of shocking conditions of near-starvation and contaminated water. Lotte couldn't help worrying that members of her own family had been locked in the camp, condemned to unimaginable squalor and suffering.

A religious woman, one morning during her prayers she was inspired to do the most extraordinary thing. She went to see the camp commandant to ask if she could deliver food parcels. The first surprise was that he agreed to see her. When he did, he told her there was no need for extra food and tried to make out that he was running a convalescent camp. During the course of this elaborate lie, he let slip that he had a son fighting in Russia. Which was when Lotte made her move: "Your son might land in a concentration camp too, and what would you say if someone were to send him an extra package of food?" In that moment, the commandant was faced with the reality that he and this Dutch woman were in much the same position. Political circumstances might have put them on opposing sides, but they were on the same side when it came to the far stronger bond of parent and child—which was why he allowed the delivery of food parcels to begin.

Not only do categorizations like "friend," "enemy," and "stranger" seem to have little meaning when they are so fragile and liable to change. Buddhism asks us to reflect more deeply about the distinction between "Self" and "Other." Other wakes up every morning, as we do, with the same wishes for security, comfort, and fulfillment. Other wants happiness and to avoid suffering in the same way as Self. Just like the German commandant and the Dutch woman, the interests of the two are synonymous—it is only force of circumstance that makes them appear any different.

This is one aspect of the Dharma with which I particularly struggle. I will see someone in the street, make an immediate, snap judgment about the kind of person they are, and immediately establish a sense of Otherness, whether positive or negative. I recognize this failing on an intellectual level, but conditioning doesn't disappear overnight, or even in the course of a few years. But slowly, we do change. At least now my snap judgments are sometimes followed by the thought that I have just made a judgment which may not be true. In breaking down the false barriers we erect between Self and Other, considering the well-being of others doesn't seem such a hopelessly idealistic objective. When we recognize we have shared hopes, this level of equanimity makes it easier to wish to help. The desire to achieve enlightenment for the sake of all beings becomes a more sincere aspiration.

The importance of being Earnest

Trevor and Jane are a young couple who've survived some very tough financial difficulties thanks to two very good friends. Ten years ago, as medical students living on government loans, their debt situation blew out completely after a car accident caused by an uninsured youth left Jane with a hefty hospital bill. Both Jane and Trevor had to take part-time jobs, a stressful situation which threatened both their studies and their relationship until Bill, their retired neighbor, stepped in. Bill had just inherited the estate of an older, wealthy brother, and was about to set off on a round-the-world journey. Sympathetic to the plight of his younger neighbors, with whom he'd always been on cordial terms, and having far more money than he knew what to do with, before he left he gave them a cash gift of such generosity that their debt was almost completely paid off. Humbled and grateful, they hardly knew how to thank Bill who, within days of making his unsolicited gift, left on his globetrotting adventure.

Seven years later, Trevor and Jane were qualified doctors. Shortly after the birth of the couple's first son, the medical group that Trevor had joined was successfully sued for malpractice. Suddenly Trevor was out of a job and once again heavily in debt through no fault of his own.

This time a golfing friend came to the rescue. Again a much older man, who thought of Trevor as the son he'd never had, Earnest offered to set Trevor up in his own practice, a position that would enable him to generate good earnings and quickly pay off his debt.

Extremely grateful, Jane and Trevor invited Earnest to their home for dinner—and thereafter they began to socialize frequently. These days the two of them can't do enough for Earnest and when their second son was born they even gave him the middle name Earnest in his godfather's honor.

But along the way there's been a strange twist to the story. Returning from his round-the-world adventure, Bill found that the lawyer to whom he'd entrusted his financial affairs had embezzled all his money and left the country without trace. Devastated and destitute, Bill soon found himself on the streets.

Jane and Trevor frequently drive or walk past where he begs

outside a supermarket—and completely ignore him. Even though their smallest gesture would make such a difference to Bill, their reaction to the shambling, wrecked old man is, at best, indifference, and more often, revulsion. In fact, they're relieved when they whiz past his squat in their BMW cabriolet and see that the police have moved him away.

While they can't do enough for Earnest, their treatment of Bill, who did just as much for them, is the total opposite. Why? Well, it's not because they're heartless monsters, or forgetful, or have developed some peculiar psychological quirk. The reason they completely ignore Bill is much simpler than that: they just don't recognize him. Bent, bearded, and broken, he looks nothing like the Bill they knew before. To them the old man outside the supermarket is just another beggar, another unwanted and unwelcome reminder of the failings of social services and the inadequacy of the welfare system. Why should they pay him any special attention?

Relationships in cyclic existence

In Buddhist terms, we are all Trevors and Janes—arguably, worse—the reason being that each one of us owes huge debts of gratitude to an inconceivable number of beings. What's more, we are now in a position to repay their kindness. But our general attitude is to drive past without even recognizing them, too wrapped up in our own preoccupations to notice or care.

On what basis does Buddhism make this startling claim? As the Dalai Lama says, "Over the billions of lifetimes that we have experienced since beginningless time, we have known all living beings again and again. Without exception each has even been a mother to us . . . how can we be indifferent to them?"

Beginningless time is one of those concepts which, in our human state, we find difficult to comprehend. Trying to imagine an age when dinosaurs ruled the world, or when all the continents were joined together, is hard enough, without traveling further back in time and space to when our known galaxy hadn't even been born. But the Buddhist view is that life, intelligent or otherwise, has always existed in a variety of realms, and in many other galaxies, so when we talk about beginningless time we shouldn't be thinking only of this realm we live in, or even this galaxy, let alone this particular planet.

The mindstream which we currently experience as you or me has also always existed. A number of analogies are used to illustrate this point. All the milk any one of us has suckled from successive mothers would be enough to fill the oceans of the world is one metaphor. Another talks of how all the bones of the successive bodies we've inhabited would tower very much higher than Mount Everest.

Following logically from this, the relationships we've had since beginningless time are infinite. However large your present name and address book is, imagine it multiplied by trillions. These trillions of relationships include a fair proportion that have been very close—parents, lovers, partners, dear friends. And just as the results we experience in our present life are not without past cause, so too our experiences with other beings are also far from random. Our difficulty is that, being Trevors and Janes, we react with indifference or even aversion to those to whom, if we only knew their identity, we would feel profoundly grateful.

Memory and rebirth

This is one of the classic arguments used in support of the practice of bodhichitta—the idea that "stranger" is actually a logical impossibility. Given our cultural conditioning, many Westerners have difficulty with the notion of rebirth, even though it's not really such a great leap. Unless you take the view that you exist as a purely biological entity, then you already accept that you have what Buddhism calls a mindstream. Exactly when that mindstream began is a question you probably can't answer using normal memory. For example, your birth is the most indisputable fact of your present existence, but can you remember it?

The argument that we couldn't have lived before because we would remember it doesn't really withstand close scrutiny. There is a clear distinction between memory and recall ability, and we all remember very much more than we are able to recall in a normal state of consciousness. It is for precisely this reason that police forces around the world use hypnosis to regress crime-scene witnesses to recall crucial details—physical descriptions, vehicle registration plates, and the like.

Hypnosis has also been extensively used for past-life regression purposes, and represents a field of mind science attracting increasing interest. Specifically, some psychologists attribute the cause of specific problems to past-life traumas which they use hypnotherapy to successfully resolve.

Having trained in hypnotherapy, I have first-hand knowledge not only of its effectiveness, but I have also had the experience of recollecting details of a previous life. More than anything, what I took away from this episode was the sheer matter-of-factness of it. There were no fireworks or shooting stars or heart-stopping revelations. I didn't feel giddy as a whole new realm of existence opened up before me. In fact, the life I remembered living three hundred years ago was so boring that I've never felt inclined to return to it. I would imagine most other people undergoing hypnotic regression would discover the same thing.

On the positive side is the recognition that the Buddhist concept of a mindstream undergoing rebirth becomes entirely plausible after an experience of this kind—and with it, the full acceptance that I have had many and varied relationships with countless other beings, who surround me in this lifetime too.

Action not belief

Because Buddhism places emphasis on action rather than belief, an intellectual understanding of concepts is important, but ultimately the only thing that counts is what we do. The Sufis have a wonderful saying which illustrates the futility of intellectual learning without practical application: "A donkey with a load of holy books is still a donkey."

Once we have weighed up the benefits of thinking about others instead of only ourselves; when we've reflected on equanimity and the artificial divide between Self and Other; after we've considered the possibility that we may have countless invisible connections to others from our previous lives—what do we do then? How are we to be wisely selfish in our everyday lives?

8. Finding Happiness in Daily Life

*In the beginning, as incipient bodhisattvas, we are not always truly
altruistic. If we claimed to be, it would just be self-deception.
But sometimes, even if only for a very short time, we understand
what we're talking about. This is why bodhichitta is so infinitely
great and so highly praised in the Mahayana sutras.*

——— TENZIN PALMO, *Reflections on a Mountain Lake* ———

NE OF THE MANY things I like about Buddhism is its practicality. Like a gigantic box of tools, it contains concepts and techniques to suit any person, in any given situation, no matter how busy, stressed out, or skeptical. The benefits of big ideas, like compassion, are set out in well-defined arguments. Following that, exactly how to apply them in day-to-day life is also clearly explained.

The Dharma speaks of "Perfections" which provide guidelines on putting bodhichitta into action. These include practices such as generosity, ethical behavior, and patience, which are mainly concerned with our interaction with the outside world. They also include instructions on how to progress on our inner journey. Combined, they provide a holistic balance.

Presented with these for the first time, you may perhaps have a sense of *déjà-vu*. Apart from the emphasis on meditation, how different are Buddhism's ideas about generosity and ethics from the basic teachings of Christianity, Judaism, or Islam?

No tradition has a monopoly on compassion, but there *is* a difference between the perfection of generosity, as described by Buddhism, and ordinary generosity. This difference can be summed up in two words: bodhichitta motivation. From a Buddhist perspective, making a gift to someone thinking, "May this act of generosity be a direct cause for all living beings, myself included, to reach enlightenment" is a very different matter from simply handing over a box of chocolates, however beautifully wrapped. The motivation is different, and the karmic results are incomparable.

As explained in the chapter on karma, motivation is one of the principal factors in determining the consequences of a particular karmic cause. The premeditated murder of one's husband in order to get one's hands on his life insurance is quite a different matter from reversing the 4WD over him by accident, even though the result for him may be the same.

So, too, the motivation of bodhichitta makes an act of generosity, ethics, or patience altogether different—even though the result for the other person may be the same.

When I first heard these teachings, I felt uncomfortable about the idea of attaching a motivation that wasn't real onto something I was planning to do anyway. Buying a cappuccino at my favorite coffee shop, to use just one example, had far less to do with a wish for all beings to become enlightened than with my need for a caffeine boost first thing in the morning. When I opened a can of cat food, I wasn't doing so to rescue all living beings from samsara, but because if I didn't, my Birman cat would sink her teeth into my ankles. It felt contrived, even false, to stick on a motivation that didn't really apply.

But recollecting this motivation throughout the day is effective psychology. It will almost certainly feel artificial at first, but fairly quickly certain actions or occasions become a trigger for the new habit and we find ourselves thinking about the enlightenment of all beings, not just when we're meditating, or reading a dharma book, but on occasions throughout the day. Keep this up for a while, and thoughts about bodhichitta become an ongoing part of our mindstream so that we begin to actively seek out opportunities for generosity, patience, and ethical behaviors. Over time, what once felt contrived becomes a heartfelt wish that influences actions of mind, body, and speech; bodhichitta motivation becomes a self-fulfilling prophecy.

The perfection of generosity

Giving is the most basic way we have of showing our concern for others. We all know the cliché about it being better to give than to receive—but why do we find it so hard to give?

Fear that we won't have enough for ourselves if we give too much away may be part of the answer, but only a small part. This is not so much an issue about our level of affluence as it is about our state of mind. My wife has a far more generous nature than I do—the difference being that she notices people in need and is more spontaneous in her response than I am. Not so long ago we went out shopping. As we walked past a supermarket, I was so deep in my own thoughts I didn't even see the elderly man struggling to lift his cart onto the pavement until Janmarie began helping him. There wasn't any lack of willingness to help on my part—I just didn't notice the need.

As busy people with demanding lives, it's easy to be so pre-occupied with our own concerns that the difficulties of others pass us by. Once again mindfulness is emphasized as a founda-tion practice.

Even when we are aware of the needs of others, we may still hold back, perhaps because we're simply not in the habit of giving. Buddhism is very pragmatic in its approach to generos-ity, suggesting that we start small and progress from there. A woman who'd been suffering from depression for months said her recovery began one day when she was at a food store. The check-out assistant made some envious comment about a bag of loose chocolates she'd just bought—so she gave her a cou-ple, then and there. The assistant's reaction to this spontaneous gift gave her such a rush of good feeling that she walked about in a glow for the rest of the day. For the first time in months she felt good about herself.

There is some good, and some bad, in all of us. What we discover when we practice generosity, even on a small scale, is that it strengthens the positive side of our nature, and rein-forces the likelihood of our acting altruistically again. It's in this altruism that our true fulfillment lies.

Christina Noble has led a remarkable life. Born and raised in Dublin, she was one of eight children with a sick mother who died when she was ten and an alcoholic father who sold his children's clothes for drink. She survived violence, sexual abuse, pregnancy, and having her baby taken away from her, all before the age of twenty.

Having experienced suffering and loss outside the experi-ence of most of us, Tina found her salvation by setting up an orphanage in Vietnam. As a middle-aged Westerner with no money, education, or powerful contacts, on a visit to Vietnam the sight—and stench—of poverty reminded her so strikingly of her own childhood she felt moved to do something to help. Walking past child beggars in the street one day she was almost overwhelmed when a little girl in rags stood up and held out her arms, not for money, but for a cuddle.

The orphanage she set up now accommodates five hundred children who pass through, and eighty permanent residents. At first regarded with suspicion by Vietnamese bureaucrats, she is now welcomed by the local police and officials who can't but recognize the value of her work.

As for Tina herself, she now feels a tremendous happiness in being alive. She has responded to the horrific experiences of her childhood with a compassion which is truly inspiring. "There are times when I'm walking down the street and one of my sunshine children shouts at me from a distance and I am so happy that I laugh and break into a skip," she says. The title of her autobiography is significant—*Bridge Across My Sorrows*. For Tina, recovery from the misery of her childhood came not from the love of a romantic partner or independence as a career woman, but through practicing generosity of the most heartfelt kind.

It is a simple but powerful truth that if we want to experience happiness, we must first give it. Generosity is the direct antidote to unhappiness. If we are too busy to practice generosity, then we're too busy to be happy—and what's the point of that?

Giving chocolates to check-out assistants, and helping old men with supermarket carts, may seem trivial in comparison with the story of Tina Noble. But if this is the fabric of our daily lives, it is what we should work with. What's important to emphasize is that it's not just the actions we take, but also the motivations which drive our behavior, that matter.

Buddhism tells us that if we reflect on the welfare of all beings without exception, then even small acts of giving take on a much greater significance. In putting out bird seed in the garden, if we think, "By this act of generosity may I, and all sentient beings, never go hungry, and may we all attain enlightenment," we have broadened the basis of our motivation far beyond the feeding of just a few birds. We have also reminded ourselves of our life's higher purpose. By doing this, even small acts of kindness have an impact on our mindstream far greater than we can imagine. More and more, on a daily basis, we help refocus our minds from Self to Other, and reprioritize our lives from the concerns of the moment to a more panoramic vision.

As you give, so shall you receive

Apart from the intrinsic benefits in the present of living with compassion, the law of karma tells us we will also enjoy very real benefits in the future.

> *Even for very rough minded beings with inferior compassion,*
> *Intent on their own purposes,*
> *Desired resources arise from giving,*
> *Causing the pacification of suffering.*

> CHANDRAKIRTI, *Engaging in the Middle Way*

Practicing generosity with material things is a cause for us to enjoy wealth in the future—even if we do so for only this reason (that is, "inferior compassion"). There are no effects without causes—by giving we create the causes for our own material well-being and, conversely, by not practicing generosity we are condemning ourselves to a future of poverty, either in this life or the next.

For Westerners, skeptical about the idea of future lives, this line of reasoning may not be very convincing. But can we be one hundred percent sure we won't have an existence after this one? Most of us wouldn't dream of driving around without car insurance, even though being involved in an accident is only a possibility. Knowing that death is a certainty, surely a little postdeath "financial planning" wouldn't go amiss?

Material giving is only one form of generosity. Buddhism also talks about giving the Dharma. As Geshe Loden explains, "The best gift that you can make to others is dharma giving because you are giving them the concepts that will enable them to obtain a lasting form of happiness . . ."

How do we set about this form of giving when we are uncertain about the Dharma ourselves? Quite simply, get to know the Dharma better. Every time we read a dharma book, meditate, or think about Buddha's teachings, we are creating limitless merit and better equipping ourselves to give dharma in the future.

We can also give protection, which means helping others out of dangerous situations. Removing an ant from your golf ball before you drive it down the fairway may seem trivial—but it's a life and death issue for the ant, and when carried out with bodhichitta motivation this simple act creates limitless merit.

I once heard a story about a woman who was rescuing starfish stranded on a beach. A whole shoal of them had washed up and, as she took her regular morning walk, she'd bend down, pick one up, and throw it back into the ocean.

"What's the point?" she was challenged by fellow walkers, overwhelmed by the enormity of the problem. "You can only save a handful."

"Yes," she agreed. "But for the handful I save, it really matters."

None of us can solve all the world's problems, but that shouldn't make us give up doing what we can to help. The amazing paradox of developing compassion and practicing generosity is the experience of just how much happiness we create for ourselves.

The perfection of ethics

Day one on your five-star African safari, and you and your friends are about to enjoy a banquet in the bush. It's lunchtime on a balmy granite outcrop. You're set up in the perfect spot—all-cane furniture, white tablecloths, and spectacular views. Everything seems perfect—until there's a commotion, and a buck suddenly comes bounding through the undergrowth. Catching sight of the group, it immediately veers left, charging back into the elephant grass.

You're a bit taken aback, but not unduly. You've already been at close quarters with far more dangerous beasts this morning, and are getting to be quite the old hand at handling African game.

But half a minute after the buck has disappeared, there's another scramble through the bush—this time it's a game warden that appears, followed by a panting, pink-faced American hunter, rifle at the ready.

"Which way did it go?" they shout.

A simple question, but answering it isn't so straightforward.

And if you're a Buddhist it could present you with a significant ethical dilemma. Do you create black karma by telling a lie? Or do you tell the truth, and assist in the likely killing of a sentient being?

This is not my ethical brain-teaser, but Buddha's, one he used to illustrate the fact that ethical issues are often far from straightforward. Which does not excuse us from trying to practice ethics, but does recognize that lists of "dos" and "don'ts" aren't always foolproof, and that there is a more important factor that should always be considered.

Buddhism encourages us to get real about ethics. While practicing the first perfection of generosity can be transformational, if generosity is combined with slippery ethics, the end result is unlikely to make us happy. So closely are the first two perfections related that they are sometimes likened to a bird's wings—both necessary to achieve lift-off.

As Buddha suggested, there is nothing straightforward about ethics, even when we try to do the right thing. In the business world, notions like corporate responsibility, triple bottom line reporting, accountability, and transparency suggest we are moving into a more ethical age. But the collapse of global accountancy firms, oil firms, and IT companies remind us how easily ethical standards can be compromised. We might like to tell ourselves we do the right thing, but sometimes it's only when a mirror is held up to our face that we are confronted by the unattractive truth.

Two creatives from an advertising agency in London were returning from lunch one day when they noticed a particularly vocal seller of *The Big Issue*—a magazine sold by homeless people to support themselves. Crossing the street to avoid him, no sooner were they back at their desks than they were told about a new pitch the agency had just won for a homelessness charity: their task was to come up with a powerful concept to persuade the public to support vendors of *The Big Issue*.

The irony of their situation wasn't lost on them. They decided to use it in a print advertisement which showed a road with the left-hand pavement crowded with pedestrians, the deserted right-hand pavement occupied only by a vendor of *The Big Issue*. The caption underneath read, "Will you choose the right side?"

Even if we want to do the right thing, we may be concerned that by adhering to high ethics we'll put ourselves in a weak situation. If we work in an industry where everyone else "exaggerates," what will become of us if *we* don't? If we reveal every source of income to the tax department, how can that possibly benefit us at the financial year end? The karmic pay-off in our next lifetime may be wonderful, but who is going to pay this year's school fees?

As with generosity, Buddhism encourages us to analyze ethics from the perspectives of both the disadvantages of nonpractice and the advantages of practice. To quote Geshe Loden, "The Buddha said that wishing for liberation but creating nonvirtue is like a blind man looking in a mirror—a pointless exercise." Just as the man's visual handicap prevents him from seeing anything in a literal sense, an ethical handicap will prevent us from seeing the truth in our dharma practice. We can spend as many hours as we like in silent meditation, but if we also engage in duplicitous activities, we might as well not bother.

The happiness that derives from ethics is not all about delayed gratification. People who are truly ethical—as opposed to merely sanctimonious—are frequently the most pleasant to be around. They are open, rather than guarded, because they don't have to conceal things. They are relaxed, free from the concern that past actions may come back to haunt them. So the happiness that comes from good ethics isn't all in the future, it is also here and now.

The practice of ethics is a vast subject within Buddhism, and includes eighteen root and forty-six branch bodhichitta vows, starting with that most universally broken injunction against praising yourself and denigrating others. However, not even this framework provides all the answers to the troubling ethical issues that underlie contemporary headlines about economic refugees, stem cell research, and nuclear waste disposal, let alone such age-old controversies as abortion and euthanasia.

Buddha did provide a useful principle, however, which he illustrated with his hunters and the buck story. In such circumstances, he said, the right ethical choice was to mislead the hunters about where the buck went in order to save its life. What really counts, he said, is motivation. The motivation to save the life of a sentient being is more important than the motivation to keep a vow of truthfulness which, in the circumstances, would have been a meaningless accomplishment.

When faced with ethical dilemmas, this is a good litmus test. What is my true motivation? Am I really concerned about the interests of the other person/being, or am I doing this for my own benefit? What if everyone in the world was to make the same choice I am considering—would this make for a happier or unhappier planet?

It is also useful to remember the distillation of Buddha's teachings—"Avoid harmfulness, cultivate goodness, subdue your mind." Even if we are faced with a situation in which we're unable to take positive action, the prevention of hurt, fear, and unhappiness is an outcome we should value.

For my own part, when faced with difficult choices, whether about ethics or other issues, I often find it helpful to imagine the Dalai Lama being presented with exactly the same choice, and I ask myself, "What would he do in the same situation?"

The perfection of patience

There is no sin like hatred,
And no tolerance like patience.
Thus, meditate on patience
Intensely with various methods.

SHANTIDEVA, *Engaging in the Bodhisattva Deeds*

Earlier we looked at the three main obstacles to happiness—attachment, anger, and ignorance. Of the three, anger, or hatred, is the most powerful—its destructive effects are said to be greater than those of any other delusion.

Patience is the direct opponent of anger, which is why Buddhists place such a high value on it. As busy people, most of us are presented with an abundance of situations in which to practice patience, but being goal-focused we see them only as things getting in our way, rather than opportunities. And it's one of the great ironies of our culture that patience is often viewed as a form of weakness. We may admire people for being generous, or ethically high-minded, or persevering to reach their goals, but how much do we admire people for their supreme patience?

Giving a shop manager a piece of our mind, letting some young lout have it with both barrels—these actions are viewed as entirely acceptable, in some circumstances admirable, in our society.

Buddhism does not advocate putting up with sloppy customer service or tolerating abusive relationships. But like the story of the buck and the hunter, what's at issue is motivation. If we are perfectly honest, we'll admit that when we tear strips off the shop manager we're not really concerned about improving service levels, though we might use that as a self-righteous excuse. We're just engaging in payback for the inconvenience he's caused. Making him squirm for all the suffering he's created. Ditto the sullen teenager whose choice in music we find so intolerable.

The big problem with anger is that once it takes hold of us, we are no longer in control. We have no idea what's going to happen next. Carried along in a tide of emotion, it's quite possible we'll say or do something that we'll regret for weeks, even years to come. Newspapers are full of such stories.

When we give in to anger, Buddhism says, we become a slave to it. We can't help ourselves because anger is in control. Far from anger being a sign of strength, we are conceding defeat over control of our own mind—and are also creating karma of the most catastrophic kind. Which, in these circumstances, is the stronger and more admirable position: caving in to raw emotions, or perfecting patience and refusing to allow our minds to be taken over?

A teacher friend of mine once told me about an eleven-year-old boy who was one of the most disruptive kids she'd ever had to deal with. A problem from his first day in class, he seemed totally out of control, and it was all she could do not to explode with anger at his insolence. Some time into term, the boy's father visited the school and explained the family circumstances. He was a single parent bringing up several kids on his own. His wife was not only estranged from the family, she was so violent he'd had to take out a restraining order to keep her away from the house and her children. Nonetheless she used to break into the house and trash the place so that when they got home in the evenings their wreck of a home would be in absolute chaos.

The son who was such trouble in my friend's class was embarrassed and upset by all this. Not only could he never invite friends around to play, he didn't even like them knowing exactly where he lived. Offered a lift home, he would always ask to be dropped several streets away—in case his mother had just visited.

After hearing this harrowing tale, my friend told me how her heart went out to the child. "The father's visit was kept confidential, of course, and I never said anything directly to him. But I think my manner must have changed. I was probably more patient in a subtle kind of way. And I kid you not, he was never a problem in my class again."

Sometimes the smallest shift in our own attitude is all we need to create change in relationships which cause us stress. It may be difficult finding the will to make concessions to those we see as aggressive and unreasonable, but just as my teacher friend experienced, even an unspoken change in attitude can be the catalyst for major transformation.

Being mindful of impatience

Recognizing the benefits of patience, both for ourselves and others, how do we go about cultivating it? The daily practice of meditation isn't a bad start. Apart from its many other benefits, meditation is a way for busy people to zero the stressometer of the mind. By reducing our overall agitation, we automatically enjoy more equanimity and tolerance. Just think how easy-going you are for the first three days after getting back from a wonderful, relaxed holiday. There's no need for this to be an annual event, however. By making meditation an everyday part of our lives, we can enjoy far greater levels of relaxation year-round.

Even with a more relaxed perspective, it's likely there will be situations in which we tend to be annoyed. Traffic. Specific work or home situations. Times of the day, the week, or the month. Having identified these contexts, we need to be extra mindful of them, as though we're entering a danger zone. Through mindfulness, the hazard lights should be flashing as we get behind the wheel of the car to drive through rush hour traffic to an important meeting. And as we sense the impatience prickling we should recollect the reality of anger: where is it coming from? Do we really want to put ourselves in a bad mood? Do we wish this cycle to be perpetuated, or are we ready to kick the habit?

And having recollected these things, it's time for the crowning moment, the perfection of patience. As things that would usually make us go crazy start to happen, we think, "For the sake of all beings, may I quickly attain the state of enlightenment by practicing patience here and now."

Having made this dedication, reflect on the advantages of perfecting patience. These are not only the present-moment benefits of retaining an inner serenity, making better judgments, and presenting a peaceful state of mind that others like to be around. There are significant karmic benefits, too. Buddhism tells us that patience is the cause for leisure and fortune. It is also the cause for others to find us an attractive person to be with.

Even the most desperate circumstances which we think can only be the cause of profound misery can, through the perfection of patience, be turned into something useful and positive. Terry Waite should know. Abducted by Hezbollah guerillas, and locked up in a series of Beirut cellars for 1,763 days, where he was subjected to physical and mental torture, he endured an experience most of us might think we'd never survive. And yet he has observed of this period. "It's been very valuable. I take the viewpoint that life is full of ups and downs, but trauma need not be totally negative. It's up to you. You can turn it around and use it constructively, which I believe I've done."

We don't need the drama of an abduction to realize the truth of this. Little by little, we work at our mindstream to eradicate unhelpful habits and create new ones. Personal transformation is a lifetime's purpose, not something we can hope to achieve in a week. But by using bodhichitta motivation, we are employing the most powerful psychology available and we shouldn't underestimate its power to change our lives for the better—sometimes in a surprisingly short time.

Meditation technique number 3:
Helping ourselves and others
The following meditation exercise, based on a practice called "Tonglen," is an exceptional way to transform our ordinary, self-focused attitude into an attitude of compassion for others. Like most meditation techniques, understanding what to do is the easy part. Practicing with heartfelt conviction and good concentration is our real challenge.

- Adopt the seven-point meditation posture. Practice a breath-counting meditation for five minutes to help calm the mind.
- Remember bodhichitta motivation. Think, "By meditating like this may I dispel all negativities, depression, and suffering that I experience, as well as the negativities, depression, and suffering experienced by all living beings. May all beings be happy, fulfilled, and quickly reach enlightenment."
- Now visualize that with each out-breath you get rid of your present and future suffering in the form of dark smoke, which you exhale. On every in-breath visualize brilliant white light entering your nostrils, streaming down your throat into your chest, and filling your entire being. The white light flushes out the dark smoke, replacing it with positive energy. Every breath of it strengthens your feeling of vibrant blissfulness, and with every exhalation the hold of negativity grows less and less. Imagine this white light has the same effect as a powerful antidepressant, except that it's both instant and completely natural.
- Repeat this process until you feel that you have exhaled all your present and future suffering, and have replaced it with a radiant, illuminating joy.
- Having dealt with your own suffering, think about those you are close to. Parents, family, good friends. Visualize them in front of you, one by one, or in groups that make sense to you, and think, "I will now get rid of any dissatisfaction or unhappiness you are experiencing now, or ever will in the future."
- As you hold a person or group in front of you in your mind's eye, continue exhaling dark smoke, but imagine you are getting rid of their suffering. As you breathe in white, positive

energy, imagine it is filling them with happiness, vibrancy, bliss.

• Once you have exhaled all the suffering of one group, and they are filled with happiness, expand the group to include others and continue the process. After friends, include strangers. After strangers, people you have difficulty with. Yes—this is a challenge! But by imagining people you usually think of as the cause of your troubles being purified of their hang-ups and mental problems, you start to find you can regard them with a greater degree of equanimity. After difficult people, include all living beings, not only humans.

• Continue the meditation for a specified time period—say ten or fifteen minutes, after which think, "I now dedicate whatever positive energy I have created through this meditation for the benefit of all beings. May we all quickly and easily attain the wonderful bliss of enlightenment."

Tonglen, the meditation practice on which this is based, is an enormously powerful tool for mind transformation. As Geshe Loden says, "Doing this meditation will eliminate the poison of self-cherishing and gorge your mind with the nectar of cherishing others. You accumulate limitless merit and quickly purify negative karma. Hindrances are overcome and you develop your realization of bodhichitta."

Living with bodhichitta

When I first learned about bodhichitta from Les at the Tibetan Buddhist Society, I had mixed feelings about the practice. While it seemed grounded in effective psychological principles, I couldn't ignore my own reservations: was it such a good idea to try remembering bodhichitta at odd times of the day when I was supposed to be focusing on other things? Could I really recollect bodhichitta without feeling like a fraud? Would practicing it really work?

By this time, Janmarie and I had been living in Perth for some time. I had grown more used to the laid-back lifestyle and the wonderful weather. Flocks of rainbow lorikeets squawking noisily in the scarlet blossoms of the bottlebrush were no longer a spellbinding novelty. Walking the expanses of the white sand beach of Cottesloe as the sun dipped below the Indian Ocean had become a normal part of our lives.

During the week I was able to work in a way that I'd only ever fantasized about. Writing in my book-lined study, or reading through a draft in the dappled sunshine of the veranda, I had realized the ambition I'd held since the age of eighteen, I was now living my dream.

Only a short while before, back in London, the very idea of such a lifestyle would have seemed hopelessly unattainable. Working in public relations, there had seemed no escape from the treadmill to which I'd felt sentenced for the rest of my working life. The thought of a twenty-second commute to work down the corridor, a phone that wasn't constantly jangling with new demands and deadlines, the freedom to live in the imaginary worlds I so loved creating—all this had seemed like something I could only ever wish for.

But now that all my hopes had been fulfilled was I happy?

Of course not! I had quickly discovered that being a full-time novelist in a Mediterranean climate isn't all it's cracked up to be!

For starters, if you're a social animal, used to a busy life, dealing with dozens of issues every day, to find your multiple tasks collapsed down to the single imperative to write 1,500 words a day is rather like hitting a brick wall at a hundred miles an hour.

Then there's the lack of a network. I was used to delivering assignments for clients on an almost daily basis, whether drafting a media release or delivering a major strategic communications plan. The result was ongoing feedback, small wins, a sense of progress. Working on a novel, however, there is almost no interaction with your peers until the entire project is over, many months later. There's no one around to provide professional support, reassurance, or encouragement.

Once again I had rediscovered the awkward truth that even when you get what you want, you find it doesn't give you all the happiness you were expecting. This time, however, I had the advantage of my dharma classes, and my weekly visits to the Tibetan Buddhist Society were a source of enormous reassurance. I regarded them then, and still do, as free psychotherapy. In fact, Lama Yeshe once wrote a book called *Becoming Your Own Therapist,* and I have yet to encounter a problem in life for which Buddhism is unable to provide practical and helpful insights.

I also discovered that the practice of bodhichitta in all its myriad forms is not only possible, but can become habitual very quickly. By associating bodhichitta motivations with some basic daily habits—making tea, going to the toilet, putting out birdseed, going to the gym—I find myself recollecting the Dharma frequently during the day. Often I find the mere reminder of a bigger picture is enough to rise above the emotion of the moment.

I have also discovered a real joy in knowing that by doing things with a more enlightened motivation I am creating huge benefits beyond the immediate task in hand. Yes, I might now have a mug of tea I didn't have a minute before, but I have also created a direct cause for all beings, myself included, to become enlightened. I have done this by conditioning my mindstream. Okay, one single thought isn't any big deal. But as quoted earlier, Buddha said, "The thought manifests as the word; the word manifests as the deed . . . As the shadow follows the body, as we think, so we become."

Every thought counts.

I have also found it is true that by shifting preoccupation away from myself and my own tiny world, the result is a higher day-to-day level of happiness. This is not a quick fix, it doesn't produce a sudden emotional high. But I have become aware of a greater sense of inner peace and contentment.

Things that have always irritated me continue to irritate me. But perhaps less intensely now, and for shorter periods of time. And when I am experiencing frustration—as I did only this morning when my computer jammed—even as I was cursing it, I couldn't avoid the foolishness of my reaction. This is samsara: what do I expect? This is my own karma coming back to haunt me. Do I want to perpetuate the cycle?

Rediscovering New York City

Even as I began making my first halting steps in the practice of bodhichitta, I was unaware that very much bigger karma was about to ripen. The paperback publication of my first novel, *Conflict of Interest,* in early 2001 was the first time I'd sensed a real momentum to my writing career. My publishers ran a light-level poster campaign on the London Underground and that, combined with good in-store promotions, saw copies of the book flying off the shelves. The long-term publishing plan seemed to be in motion. *Pure Deception* was launched simultaneously in hardback. But best of all, my third novel, *Expiry Date*, which I was particularly excited about, had been greeted with much enthusiasm, not only by my editor, but also by a new agent in New York.

In just a short space of time I seemed to have come a very long way. I had made the journey from wage-slave in a PR agency to novelist published around the world, and now had the prospect of an American deal. I knew that with a New York publishing contract behind me, things in Hollywood could fall into place a lot easier. I always knew my books to be very visual and had been told by readers on countless occasions that they could easily imagine them as movies. Was I about to make the breakthrough to a fully global readership?

I decided to visit my New York agent to talk about what happened next. The day of our meeting I began the day, as usual, with a meditation session in my hotel room, before catching the elevator to the penthouse floor dining room. As I got into the elevator, shortly before 9:00 A.M., a fellow hotel resident caught my eye. "Have you seen the news?" she asked. "Someone's just flown a plane into the World Trade Center."

I was surprised, naturally, but not unduly alarmed. I imagined some light aircraft had accidentally flown off-course.

As we stepped out onto the penthouse floor, however, a very different story was emerging. Instead of the usual hubbub that accompanied breakfast, everyone was staring, transfixed, at the single TV monitor. Like every other news monitor in the world it was showing live images of the devastation occurring to the first World Trade Center tower. Then that apocalyptic icon of the jet plunging directly into the second.

Most of us can remember where we were when we heard about September 11. When I tell people I was in New York City, they often react as though I was caught up in the middle of a war zone. But the more prosaic reality was that had I not ventured out of my hotel, the whole thing might have been happening in a different city. Looking outside as the surreal drama unfolded, I remember thinking what a beautiful autumn day it was, the sky so blue and cloudless.

It was to be some hours before the full scale of the Al-Qaeda attack was known or understood. While today the simple sequence "9/11" conveys instant and profound significance, on the morning itself most people in New York were far more concerned with simple practicalities. How much damage had been done to the financial district? Were they expected in at work? Was the subway still running?

During this strange nethertime, I met with my New York agent. She repeated her enthusiasm for *Expiry Date* and listed the publishers she was keen to try. But there could be no escaping the events unraveling just a few miles away—they completely overshadowed our meeting.

One of the worst things about being on the edge of disaster is the terrible sense of utter helplessness. After my meeting, I returned to the hotel for the latest news update. Despite the near-miraculous escape of so many people from the World Trade Center, the appalling casualties were already apparent. What could one do to assist? TV and radio announcements had summoned medical assistance but asked other volunteers to stay away from Ground Zero. Within minutes of asking for blood donors, hospitals were overwhelmed with so many volunteers that they put out a request for no more.

Out on the streets were the most extraordinary sights as all the traffic headed away from the disaster zone. Most notice-ably, pedestrians trudged uptown to find their way to the near-est functioning subway. The only traffic heading south was emergency vehicles.

And during the course of all this pandemonium, New York changed. Or perhaps showed its true colors. Mobile phones were willingly offered by people who'd never met to help others make contact with loved ones. Businessmen wearied from a thirty-block hike were invited into apartments for a drink by perfect strangers. Information, car rides, even free accommodation were offered to those who found themselves in difficulty.

By mid-afternoon an eerie stillness had settled over the Upper West Side. Almost all businesses had closed down, their doors papered with hastily printed notices. Residents remained indoors, focused on the TV images. The constant wailing of ambulances and fire engines was a continuing reminder of the unfolding drama on the south of the island. The air had turned bitter with smoke.

Unable to remain cooped up in my room, in the early eve-ning I went for a walk along the near-deserted streets close to the hotel. There were a few people around but not many. I passed a man walking his dog and we exchanged eye contact and hellos. It was only afterwards I realized what an extraordi-nary event that was for New York.

Very few restaurants were open, and not a single café. Con-templating the unappealing prospect of room service, just a couple of blocks south of the hotel I came across a venue which was a coffee shop by day and club by night. Call it the power of free enterprise, or a gutsy spiritedness, but not only had this business remained open, the staff were out on the pavement offering free coffees and inviting in passers-by.

I required no second invitation. Of course, by that stage very few people were interested in coffee, free or otherwise. Ordering some wine, I was soon at a packed table with a whole bunch of other people who didn't know each other, trading stories of the day. Quite a few of us were out-of-towners here on business. There was the vehicle-leasing executive from Chicago, the jewelry importer from Vancouver, two Italian students on a Fine Art study trip, and a twitchy local woman with a moth-eaten spaniel.

With the whole of the city seeming to have closed down around us, that little bar felt like the village hall. Outside the streets were empty and acrid. But inside we listened to the group that had taken to the small stage with a medley of pop classics.

At some point in the evening I remember a rendition of "American Pie." Several drinks on, a number of the audience joined in, until the whole of that small café was singing. It was a spontaneous and heartfelt response, and one which seemed entirely right for the time. United in Don McLean's famous anthem of loss, we all knew we had said goodbye to something that day—but exactly what remained to be seen. Complacency? Innocence? Certainties that could no longer go unchallenged?

For my own part, I had no idea just how directly the consequences of September 11 would affect me. Within months my world would be turned upside down. Singing along with the rest of them, little did I realize how prophetic the lyrics of that song would prove to be—just how much that was the day the music died.

9. The Heart of Buddha's Wisdom

Enlightenment is the moment the wave realizes it is water.
At that moment, all fear of death disappears.

——— THICH NHAT HANH, *The Heart of Understanding* ———

F ALL THE BUDDHA's teachings, the wisdom of "dependent arising" is the subtlest and the most revolutionary. So dramatic are its implications for the way we see ourselves and the world around us that there is an established tradition not to reveal this ancient and life-changing truth to those who are not yet sufficiently mature to grasp it. For this reason, dependent arising always appears towards the end of Lam Rim teachings.

First, to provide some context, Buddhism is often known as "the Middle Way." This metaphor works on a number of different levels. The highest of these, which concerns us now, seeks to describe how the Buddhist tradition avoids the two extremes of nihilism and eternalism.

The nihilist view is that all beings can be explained adequately and only in terms of flesh and blood, nature and nurture, genes and environment. Our brains equal our minds and when we die, that's all folks, thank you and goodnight.

As busy people, for the most part this materialist model accords quite well with our experience of reality. But there are some awkward phenomena which aren't so easily accounted for. How is it that, on an ongoing basis, clairvoyants are effortlessly able to provide intimate details about people, both living and dead? How are some people's telepathic skills so powerful that intelligence agencies have been known to recruit "remote viewers"? Why are some of us able to recall, under hypnosis, astounding historical facts to which we could never possibly have had access? What of ghosts, miracle healings, religious experiences like stigmata, near-death experiences both positive and negative, not to mention a host of other supernatural phenomena?

The nihilist view is to dismiss all these as clever hoaxes, coincidences, mind over matter, or wishful thinking. Unable to account for them in materialist terms, their existence is denied or derided.

At the other end of the spectrum, the eternalist view is that we have within us a soul or spirit, often thought of as the "real me" or "essential me." When we die this soul goes to heaven, hell, or purgatory, where it may well have the good fortune to run into the souls of departed former friends and loved ones from planet Earth. Alternatively, in some eastern traditions, the soul may be propelled into a new reincarnation as a result of karma.

Exactly what constitutes this "real me" or "soul" is not a question which eternalists are able to answer with any certainty. Which is paradoxical, given the overwhelming importance of this purported entity. And there are fundamental questions, the answers to which are unclear. For example, we know that if someone suffers damage to different parts of their brain, they will lose their memory, or their personality will dramatically alter. Given that memory and personality are brain functions, what are we left with when at our death our brain dies? Do souls have memory or personality? If so, are these functions independent of the memory and personality residing in the brain?

The Buddhist view is that neither nihilism nor eternalism accords with a dispassionate analysis of reality, and that the truth lies between these two points—hence "the Middle Way." This can pose a challenge for Westerners, especially when presented with these teachings for the first time. Our binary minds tell us that you can't have it both ways. It's either a 1 or a 0, nihilist or eternalist —there are no other possibilities.

But Buddhism encourages us to be a little more sophisticated in our thinking. It is not merely the existence or nonexistence of phenomena which is at issue here. It is, critically, *how* phenomena exist.

Understanding the answer to this question is far more than an interesting academic abstraction. It is the ultimate goal of all Buddhist philosophy, and our personal experience of it leads us directly to enlightenment.

How things exist

Reality is an illusion, albeit a persistent one.

ALBERT EINSTEIN

Buddha explained that all things exist merely as dependent arisings. Specifically, all phenomena are dependent on causes, parts, and mental projection. This may seem a fairly straightforward assertion, but its implications are worth looking at.

Causes

Buddhist monk Thich Nhat Hanh opens his beautifully written book *The Heart of Understanding* with these lines:

> If you are a poet, you will see clearly that there is a cloud floating in this sheet of paper. Without a cloud, there will be no rain; without rain, the trees cannot grow; and without trees, we cannot make paper. The cloud is essential for the paper to exist.

He goes on to describe how the sun, the soil, the logger, the logger's parents, and a myriad of other elements were all required to create the sheet of paper. Without any one of them, the paper could not exist.

Each of us, too, is evolving amid a vast range of interdependent relationships: we are dependent on causes. Our parents, who conceived us. The influences of childhood experiences on our minds and bodies. The media we consume and people we spend our time with. Right now, as busy people in the early twenty-first century, we exist more interdependently with the rest of the world than we ever have before.

I sometimes reflect how, on an ordinary weekday, I have already relied on tens of thousands of relationships right around the world even by the time I get to my desk at half past eight in the morning. I wake up in a bed that was manufactured in Australia, using components from several different countries. Apart from the manufacturer, and the retailer from whom we bought the bed, there were the various employees within those organizations who had a part in the manufacture of this particular bed, the suppliers of all the constituent parts of the bed, the transport workers who brought it to our home, the bank managers who financed all those companies enabling them to operate, the service staff such as accountants, HR, and marketing executives who made them run effectively. All of them had parents, many from other countries, and a multitude of influences which brought them to the period when, about six years ago, they had a role to play in the assembly, sale, and delivery of our particular bed.

We haven't even considered the sheets, pillows, and blankets yet. In fact, I haven't even got out of bed. What about all the stuff in the bathroom and kitchen? The Colombian coffee and the muesli with ingredients from half a dozen different countries?

We mostly tend to think of ourselves as individuals who exist quite separately from the rest of the world. But as even this rudimentary analysis shows, in reality we are extremely dependent on vast numbers of people and events at any one moment. We don't so much exist as coexist. Take out one component part, and the whole picture changes.

It's all very well saying that many of these relationships are so subtle that they're hardly worth considering. So what if the Zulu family in South Africa hadn't sent their son to the mine from which he drilled the iron ore required for the steel bolt which now holds the frame of your bed together? Wouldn't you have slept just as soundly with another bolt or in another bed? Of course—but you would only be exchanging one set of interdependent relationships with another. And from the most subtle and removed, to the most powerful and direct, these relationships cause us to be who we are.

Some people bristle at the suggestion that they are in any way influenced by others. They pride themselves on having firm, and often contrary, views, formed on the basis of rational analysis and nothing else besides. As a communications professional I never fail to be amused by the results of research surveys in which people claim not to be influenced by advertising. On what basis, I wonder, do they think billions of dollars are spent on promotional campaigns every year? The advertising industry only thrives because it is so successful at changing attitudes and behavior.

Like it or not, we are all constantly being influenced by people around us. The very fact we can communicate is only because of the language we have all learned from others. Every word we use originally came from someone else. And because the influences on us are constantly changing, so are we.

Most of us know stories along the lines of the hard-nosed businessman who, having had a brush with death, is visited at a vulnerable moment by a priest, and subsequently becomes a devout churchgoer and philanthropist. The drug-addicted adolescent who watches his best friend die of an overdose, and resolves to get clean. Or, in a less dramatic but no less profound way, the conversation we've had with someone from a group for which we usually have little sympathy that makes us question our previous attitudes.

As the people and influences around us change, we change too. Dependent on causes, the only thing of which we can be certain is that in ten, five, or even two years' time we will be a different person from the one we are today.

Parts

Buddha also taught that all things are dependent on parts. Of the three aspects of dependent arising, this is probably the most obvious, the easiest to understand. Without a motor, a car is not a car. Without petals, a flower is not a flower.

As individuals, on what parts are we dependent? Anyone who has read Christopher Reeve's poignant autobiography, *Still Me,* cannot help being moved by the plight of the former Superman actor who became unable to move so much as an arm. In his own mind he was still "me." But because of a single horse-riding accident, even though we may admire his emotional resilience, to his fans he was no longer Superman. The preaccident Christopher Reeve was a completely different being.

Still more dramatic is the story of former magazine editor Jean-Dominique Bauby. In his autobiography, *The Diving Bell and the Butterfly,* he describes how a serious stroke at the age of forty-three reduced him to a condition in which he was "locked" in an immovable body, able to control only the blinking of his left eyelid. Through this means alone he painstakingly dictated his entire book, letter by letter. Like Christopher Reeve, Jean-Dominique Bauby's active life came to an abrupt halt. His mental continuum was the same, but the basis on which he existed was completely different.

While, on a gross level, it is easy to see that all entities depend for their existence on a number of functioning component parts, on a more subtle level it is significant that, as Thich Nhat Hanh puts it, "this sheet of paper is made up only of 'nonpaper elements.' And if we return these nonpaper elements to their sources, then there can be no paper at all." We may be David, Susan, or Jeff, but we consist entirely of non-David, non-Susan, and non-Jeff components. Even the DNA which has a critical role to play in our apparent David-ness, Susan-ness, or Jeff-ness consists entirely of non-David, non-Susan, and non-Jeff elements.

Just as the causes on which we depend are constantly

changing, so too are the parts. Growth and entropy ensure that nothing lasts forever. Computers crash, fruit rots, and hell-raising teenagers become feeble geriatrics.

The changes we notice the least are in ourselves. When we stare in the mirror, we look just the same as ever. But pull out a photograph from ten or twenty years ago and we are stopped short by the dramatic difference. How could all that have passed by without our noticing?

At a cellular level, our bodies are constantly regenerating, from the fresh skin cells manufactured daily to the slow-growth cells of our bones. In seven years' time, our entire body will have completely regenerated and we won't possess a single cell that we do today. One story I've always liked tells of a prisoner who wrote to the Supreme Court demanding to be released on the basis that, after seven years, he was no longer the same person who had committed the crime!

Mental projection

Rod and Jim are the best of friends. They grew up together, were groomsmen at each other's weddings, socialize regularly, and know everything there is to know about each other.

Today they are sitting together, watching events unfold before them. Both are drinking the same brand of beer and eating the same kind of meat pie. Their vantage is as close as you can get to identical, and for a full ninety minutes neither of them is exposed to any individual stimulus.

After ninety minutes have gone by, Rod is euphoric, beaming from ear to ear and pumping the air with his fist, while Jim is so dejected that even the prospect of the journey home exhausts him. Having been on the receiving end of exactly the same external reality, how is it possible that the two of them have been propelled into such strikingly different emotional states?

The answer, if you haven't already guessed it, is quite simple. They are supporters of rival football teams, and Rod's team has just thrashed Jim's.

There is nothing remarkable about this story. Versions of it are played out at every moment around the planet, where the same events are provoking entirely different reactions from different people. Most of us have no difficulty at all with the idea that external events don't automatically dictate an internal response—just as long as our own minds or emotions aren't engaged. As dispassionate observers, we can see quite clearly how two people can have different, even opposing, interpretations of the same event, whether it's a football match, a kiss, or the terms of a business deal. It's quite obvious to us that the external event itself is not the cause of their very different reactions, that it's their beliefs and attitudes—their mental projection—which make them react in a particular way.

When we are the center of the action, however, it's a very different story. We find it hard to see that there could be any other interpretation besides our own for what has happened, much less accept that other interpretation.

The wiping out of thousands of innocent civilians by aircraft controlled by hate-filled people strikes us as an unprovoked and barbaric outrage. So too did it strike the residents of Hiroshima. While we may have been disgusted by Islamic fundamentalists celebrating September 11, we tend not to remember the celebrations by Allied forces after the dropping of the first atomic bomb in 1945.

Beliefs vs. real-life events

In my twenties, I suffered from enormous depression, arising, I believed, from having been dumped by my girlfriend. In the highly militarized environment in which I grew up, this was known as "taking a bullet," and one of my university yearbooks has a cartoon showing me riddled with machine gun fire.

I regarded myself as having little choice in the way I responded to an event which was also certainly not of my choosing. All I wanted was for us to get back together again—a possibility that didn't exist.

Unable to work my way out of this unhappy situation, it was only when a highly skillful therapist, Bob "Super" Hooper, asked me to write down a list of all the reasons why "taking a bullet" made me feel so depressed that things began to change. Using a form of cognitive therapy practiced in the West since the 1960s (and in the East since the sixth century B.C.), the therapist explained that "real-life events" don't automatically make you feel a particular way. It's your interpretation of those events—your mental projection—which produces the feelings.

Even while writing the list, having to commit my interpretations to paper, I began to experience doubts. In the next session, Super Hooper asked me to hand the list over, and proceeded to demolish every single reason with a compelling *tour de force* of irresistible humor and logic.

"You say you'll never meet anyone like Tracy again?" he challenged. Then, with a mischievous grin, "Sounds to me like you wouldn't want to. But tell me, how old are you?"

"Twenty-one."

"And what age do most people you know get married, or move in together?"

I shrugged. "Mid-twenties, early thirties."

"You only dated a couple of girls before you met Tracy, right?"

I nodded.

"And you're seriously trying to tell me that even if you carry on dating for another ten years, you'll never find a compatible partner?!"

When you go to the therapist, you expect kid gloves and Kleenex, not debating class. But Super Hooper was exactly what I needed—someone to challenge my persistent self-destructive beliefs. After a few rounds in the ring with him, it became more and more difficult to remain depressed for very long. I'd start to feel overwhelmed by the familiar sinking sensation and then I'd think: *Hang on! What am I getting depressed about?*

There was no question of completely eradicating every last bit of unhappiness over what had happened—I am human. But it was as though the rug had been pulled from beneath my depressive feelings. Having looked at them closely, I knew they were founded on fraud. As Super Hooper never failed to point out, the reasons for my unhappiness were all in my head. Not every twenty-one-year-old who "takes a bullet" dissolves into chronic depression. I did have some choice in the matter. I could lighten up a little, just for a start!

Our life, our projection

Taking together the different elements on which all things depend—causes, parts, and mental projection—what becomes apparent is that the model of reality most of us work with is, in fact, fundamentally flawed. For as long as we can remember, we've had a sense of a concrete, separate world out there with which we as concrete, separate individuals interact.

But this "solid state" version of reality has been long discredited by scientists. It is fascinating that contemporary quantum physics describes the nature of reality in a way that resonates strongly with the teachings of a man who lived two and a half thousand years ago. Buddhist concepts of karma and dependent arising have direct parallels to the basic scientific view that the universe is a field of constantly changing energy and matter.

Buddha and the scientists agree that there's not a concrete, permanent, or independent thing in the entire universe. Such an entity is incapable of existing. *Everything* is interdependent and in a state of ongoing flux.

It is exactly because all phenomena are dependent arisings that they are often described as empty of self-existence. But because they are empty of self-existence, they are dependent arisings. These are two sides of the same coin.

Where the concept of dependent arising starts to get *really* interesting is when we apply it to the person we think of as "me."

The nature of "me"

By holding "self," we hold "other."
Through "self and other," attachment and aversion arise.
And in connection with this
All faults occur.

DHARMAKIRTI, *Commentary on the*
Compendium of Valid Cognition

In the last chapter we looked at how Self is the cause of our dissatisfaction. It is Self who believes we ought to enjoy a certain lifestyle, or the love of others, or a position of influence, or sensual gratification, or all the above. We all walk around with quite firmly entrenched ideas about ourselves, including our life stories, our personal preferences, our strengths and weaknesses. These all contribute to a solid sense of "I."

In the chapter on Buddha's First Teaching we also looked at the paradox of narcissism, how self-focusing leads not to happiness but to unhappiness. The practice of bodhichitta is one direct opponent to this. But another, ultimate opponent is dependent arising.

For when we apply dependent arising to Self, what we find is that this apparently powerful, concrete, and critically important Self simply doesn't exist—not as an independent entity. The harder we look, the more we find that there's no such being. We're making the whole thing up. Self is nothing more than a figment of our imagination!

How do we know this to be true? Because the idea we have of ourselves is no one else's. We may believe we have certain characteristics or qualities. But if a poll were conducted of all who know us, including family members, partners, and ex-partners, would every single one of those people agree? Do others see us the way we see ourselves? Would even our nearest and dearest provide a coherent picture?

It was precisely this dilemma that drove Scottish poet Robbie Burns to ask, "O wad some Pow'r the giftie gie us/To see oursels as others see us!" ("Oh, would some power had the gift to give us/To see ourselves as others see us!"). It's amazing how much energy many of us spend worrying about the impression we have made on other people, how they thought we came across, what sort of image we have.

In reality, the idea we have of ourself exists in our mind alone. Nobody else shares it, nor do they really care, because they have their own projection of us. What's more, even our own projection is highly conditional on our mood. When we're depressed, our failings and inadequacies can seem overwhelming. In an upbeat mood, we sometimes find a whole lot to be positive about. Over time, our idea of who we are also changes; our values, our hopes, who and what we hold near and dear to us are all very fragile. So which of all these different versions of ourselves is "the real me?"

The two "I's"

Buddhism talks of the two "I's." The first "I" is a label of convenience which we apply to our psycho-physical continuum. Sure, the continuum may have moved on from what it was yesterday or ten years ago. And sure, your experience of it may be very different from mine. But in the absence of any better alternative, we call this constantly changing collection of non-I elements "me," "myself," "I." This version of "I," which takes into account dependent arising, is the correct one.

But most of us go a step further. On top of this constantly changing collection of non-I elements, we project an "I" which doesn't actually exist. This false "I" is a possessor and controller. "My legs were aching but I felt elated" might not strike us as a peculiar thing to say. But what's going on here? Who is this "I" that feels elated? The way we put it, it's as though the legs belong to this "I," in much the same way as an umbrella or a set of keys. They are incidental to the elation currently felt by "I." But, as we've already seen, there is no such thing as an "I" that owns anything. "I" is merely a collection of parts, including legs.

The false or projected "I" has such a strong hold over our

minds, nonetheless, that we are convinced that this owner or controller really exists. Not only that, we project all kinds of characteristics onto him or her.

Just as we project certain things onto the outcome of a football match, the dropping of a bomb, the ending of a relationship, so too we project all kinds of things onto this constantly changing collection of non-I elements and proceed to convince ourselves that our projections are real. "I" am an introvert. "I" believe in green causes. "I" don't have a head for figures.

Lama Yeshe used to talk about the "double bubble" that we all walk around inside. The first bubble is the false "I," the apparently self-existent, independent "I" that we project. The second bubble comprises all the qualities we project onto this nonexistent "I." The reason he chose the bubble analogy is that the projections are so easily popped.

Where our projections come from

Where do we come up with these projections in the first place? They arise, in brief, through karma. Different people see the same thing, hear the same music, sense the same fragrance in very different ways because they come to these things with different conditioning.

We begin our lives with the nature/nurture bundle arising from previously created karma. And from a myriad of possibilities as we grow, the interplay of causes and conditions ripens our karma in such a way that we project our idea about the way things exist onto the outside world and onto ourselves.

As we've already seen, there is no such thing as a concrete, self-existent world out there. If there were, we would all agree on how it exists. It is precisely because all phenomena, including ourselves, are dependent arisings that we all have such different ideas about the way they exist. In this way, karma and dependent arising go hand in hand.

We are extremely fortunate to experience reality in this way, because if we don't like our projection, we can change it. Karma, like everything else, is merely a dependent arising. Change the karma and we change the way that life seems. With every act of body, speech, and mind, we are inventing our future reality.

If not my Self, who am I?

The sense of self, of ego or I, is not the same thing as consciousness; it is a form that consciousness takes under certain conditions which in man are connected with the senses and the complex organization of forces and substances that make up the human body.

LOBSANG P. LHALUNGPA, *The Life of Milarepa*

You may at this point be thinking, "Well, that's just great! Having demolished the idea of 'me' that I've been walking around with for the past X years, what exactly are you leaving me with? And what remains when I die? Nothing?!"

As Lobsang Lhalungpa makes clear in the quotation above, abandoning the false sense of "I" or "me" doesn't negate the existence of consciousness. It only negates a demonstrably false model of consciousness.

What we are left with after abandoning the false "I" is consciousness, or mindstream, propelled by karma. A mindstream that will undergo pleasant and unpleasant experiences, that may be reborn as a malnourished dog in an African village or a bouncing bundle of joy to wealthy parents in California—all depending on karma. The choice is ours.

But a far more tantalizing prospect is that of a consciousness that has transcended samsara. An awareness which is no longer propelled by karma. This consciousness has been within us since beginningless time and is sometimes described as our Buddha nature. The experience of it is nirvana.

At the beginning of this chapter I quote Thich Nhat Hanh, who describes enlightenment as what happens when the wave realizes it is water. It is a wonderful metaphor, describing what happens when we abandon the false construct of the Self as an independent, separate "I," and discover that our own true nature is pure, primordial, boundless awareness, at one with the universe. Our first experience of this naturally abiding quality or character is the discovery of the emptiness of our own self-existence. We begin to understand the illusory nature of appearances.

Buddha talked a great deal more about dissatisfaction than he did about what it feels like to be enlightened, giving as his reason that most of us can't even begin to imagine this state of blissful awareness. Enlightened masters have subsequently told us that nothing we experience as humans, not even the most ecstatic state of orgasm, can come close to the bliss of enlightenment. It is also true that many practitioners who have enjoyed a certain level of success in their meditation show the greatest reluctance to come out of retreat.

The phrase "oceanic experience" describes something that many people have had glimpses of—unexpected instants when they feel part of a blissful, much greater energy. Given Thich Nhat Hanh's wave analogy, this term for immense, radiant happiness seems highly appropriate.

With at least a theoretical understanding of our true, primordial nature, we can see how death is a result of our false belief in self-existence. It arises from a misconception of "I." For in reality, there is nothing to die. There never was. The wave's true nature always was water. If it thought any differently, it was the victim of self-limiting beliefs!

According to the *Tibetan Book of the Dead*, "The true nature of things is void, spacious, and naked as the sky. The clear light of emptiness, without a center or a circumference, is the dawning of awareness of pure consciousness." In recognizing that a self-existent "I" doesn't exist, we understand our true nature. We experience bliss.

Putting dependent arising into practice

Merely suspecting emptiness causes samsara
to be torn asunder.

ARYADEVA

Dependent arising is a slippery concept. No sooner have you got a firm grip of it than—*eek!*—it's eluded your grasp, and you're left knowing that reality isn't quite as it seems, but unsure about exactly how or why. Because dependent arising, and the flipside concept of emptiness, go against all our previous conditioning, most of us need to hear teachings on the subject again and again just to form a stable, conceptual understanding of it.

It's worth noting that, because this is the heart of Buddhism, many books have been written and teachings given which don't always use the same terminology. Other terms commonly used when discussing this subject are "special insight" and "shunyata wisdom."

"Emptiness," short for "emptiness of self-existence," is probably the most used term for what, as we've already seen, is the natural corollary to dependent arising: because phenomena depend on parts, causes, and mental projection, they are empty of self-existence. Because they are empty of self-existence, they are dependent on parts, causes, and projection.

The reason I've focused on dependent arising rather than emptiness in this explanation is because most of us use "emptiness" and "nothingness" interchangeably in daily life. When reflecting on the Dharma, however, if you were to think that emptiness means nothingness you would be committing a basic error and be guilty of nihilism!

At a conceptual level, dependent arising can come as a thrilling, eye-opening discovery to even the most jaded of cynics. As with everything else in Buddhism, however, it's not what you think, it's what you *do* that counts. So important is our direct, personal experience of dependent arising, particularly in a deep meditative state, that all Buddha's teachings are said to lead directly or indirectly to this goal.

As Milarepa, the famous Buddhist yogi and poet, said, "Just as a starving man cannot be fed by the knowledge of food but needs to eat, so too one needs to experience in meditation the meaning of emptiness."

In earlier chapters we have seen how renunciation is symbolized in the lotus flower, and bodhichitta in a moon (silver-colored) cushion. Dependent arising or emptiness is symbolized by a sun (gold-colored) cushion on which images of Buddhas are often seen to be sitting. In order, the awakened Buddha sits on a sun cushion, on top of a moon cushion, on top of a lotus blossom.

Just as the lotus is a metaphor for our ability to achieve transcendence despite the muck in which we are rooted, and the

moon cushion is emblematic of the serene beauty of bodhichitta, the sun cushion equates to the radiance we experience
when we realize dependent arising at a non-conceptual level.
The phrase "lotus, moon, and sun" is often used to describe the
Buddhist path.

Earlier, we looked at the experience of being in love, and
how no Harlequin romance, slushy pop song, or Hollywood
confectionery can in any way compare to the actual feeling of
being in love.

So too with dependent arising. No amount of hypothetical
conjecture can substitute for experiencing the real thing. Given
that this experience, the ultimate goal of Buddhism, is beyond
anything we as humans are capable of imagining, beyond concept, beyond words, how do we set about achieving it?

As much as I'd like to write from personal experience, like
most practitioners I have to rely on the wisdom of the most
advanced meditators. They tell us that before any direct experience, we should get very familiar with the concept of dependent arising. By thoroughly acquainting ourselves with the idea,
by reminding ourselves throughout the day that everything we
experience is merely dependent arising, gradually our percep-
tion of ourselves, and the world around us, begins to shift.

The two-pronged method

One method I particularly like combines the reminder of bodhichitta and dependent arising in a powerful double-whammy.
The technique is extremely flexible and can be adapted to a
huge variety of situations. It's also quick enough to be used by
busy people on the run, quite literally from the moment you
wake up to the moment you go to sleep.

First thing in the morning, stepping into the shower, as the warm water blasts onto my face, I think, "By this act of purification, may I and all beings quickly achieve enlightenment." This thought is followed up with the reminder, "I am merely a dependent arising. The act of showering is merely a dependent arising. All things are merely dependent arisings."

Minutes later, taking a first sip of morning coffee is an opportunity to dedicate an act of regeneration for the benefit of all beings, while once again recollecting the true nature of coffee, self, and everything else.

In the last chapter we discussed how we can turn mundane activities into transcendent ones when we remember bodhichitta motivation. By recollecting dependent arising as well, this practice becomes immeasurably more beneficial because we are countering the mistaken view of reality we've had since birth.

We can apply the double-whammy method not only to situations of generosity, patience, and ethical restraint, but to any ordinary activity. Brushing our teeth. Going to the gym. Mailing a letter. No matter what situation presents itself, we have the tools to turn it into a step closer to our awakening.

"Isn't this all a bit complicated?" you may be wondering. "Surely life is busy enough without having to get your mind around all that stuff?"

If we're honest, however, we'll admit that most of what goes through our minds on such occasions contributes little, if anything, to our well-being. Why not replace the usual fragmented meanderings with something more useful? On some occasions, when we're in a hurry, we may not have much time for extended practice. But we should try to use other occasions as an opportunity for a mini-analysis.

For example, instead of listening to some vacuous breakfast show on the car radio on our way to work, a more karmically beneficial alternative would be to think, "By this act of going into work to earn a living, to support myself and those who depend on me while I practice the Dharma, may all beings be freed from suffering and quickly achieve enlightenment.

"At the same time, the reality is that I, the organization I work for, and the work I do are merely dependent arisings. There is nothing inherently existent about any of us. We all depend on causes, parts, and mental imputations. We have no existence outside those things.

"So I'm going to relax! I won't get sucked into the fallacy of samsara! I recognize that I exist only as a part of a boundless, interdependent universe. And that being the case, how better to dedicate whatever merit I accumulate from my work than as a cause for all living beings, myself included, to achieve enlightenment?"

The thought may be occurring to you that while this kind of practice may be useful from a dharma perspective, what about its impact in other ways? If I wander about the place thinking about bodhichitta and dependent arising all the time, will I start to lose my grip on reality? Will I lose my competitive edge? Will I start to underperform?

Actually, the reality on which we have such a firm grip is just an illusion; if anything, we are only just beginning to get a grip on true reality! But quite apart from that, the experience of most practitioners I know has been improved performance in the world, not the opposite.

As we learned from Mr. Piña Colada earlier in the book, a level of non-attachment is very helpful in our work. If we want to get ahead, make money, or operate effectively, doing so in an unemotional and objective manner is likely to enhance our chances. As calm people, at peace with our non-self-existent selves, we are not only capable of drawing more enjoyment from the process, we are also better able to see the big picture. And it is also the case that people are drawn to others who are calm and practice good ethics and can find it in their hearts to respond with compassion.

As busy people, most of us do a lot of thinking. Far too much of it. Acquainting our very congested mindstreams with the concept of dependent arising is a good analytical way to effect change. But the complement to this is an experiential method which we can achieve through meditation.

Meditation technique number 4:
Mahamudra
The mahamudra meditation method involves having our own mind as the object of meditation. It is a profound subject on which entire books have been written and which should ideally be practiced under the direction of an experienced teacher.

Nonetheless, even a fairly superficial experience of mahamudra can be a useful way of making real the concepts described in this chapter:

- Adopt the seven-point meditation posture.
- Practice a breath-counting meditation to calm the mind. Take special care to focus all your attention on the sensation of the breath entering and leaving your nostrils.
- After your mind has become more settled, turn the focus of your attention to the mind itself.
- As thoughts inevitably arise, avoid becoming caught up in them. Just think, "A thought about my bank balance has just arisen," and let go of the thought. It is surprising how

quickly such thoughts will disappear if we don't empower them. But this goes against most of our usual mental behavior, which is to become caught up with abstractions.

- In between arising thoughts, focus on the spacious peacefulness of your mind. This is rather like seeing the expansive sky after obscuring clouds have blown away. See how long you can hold on to just the wonderful, unobscured clarity of it.

- As your concentration improves with practice, you will find fewer and fewer thoughts arising, and more and more absence of thought. The tone of your meditation will become more quiet and radiant.

- Very frequently, a bad session will follow a good one. Don't worry. At the end of a bad session take comfort in the fact that by recognizing the turbulence of your mind you were at least being mindful of mind.

These are the very basics of mahamudra. In experimenting with this meditation method you may very well feel like the survivor of a shipwreck caught in a turbulent ocean—I certainly do sometimes. But a meditation method that starts out as being very difficult can, with persistence, become a source of enormous calm. Instead of disruption, one may experience just some of the boundless radiance of our primordial minds. In fact, returning to the room at the end of the session can come as a disappointment. It is these small victories which keep us moving towards our ultimate objective.

In praise of dependent arising

Know that all appearances are like a dream,
Illusionary projections of your mind.
Grasping nothing, beyond all concepts,
Rest in the wisdom of pure consciousness.

TSELE NATSOK RANGDROL

My dharma teacher, Les Sheehy, has a particularly impactful way of getting across the message of dependent arising. Sitting on his teaching throne—a slightly raised platform next to a Buddha statue at the front of the class—he will reach over and remove a bloom from one of the flower offerings, arranged by students in vivid abundance.

"Is this a flower?" he will ask the class, to general agreement.

Then, removing a single petal, he will hold it up. "Is this a flower?"

To solemn head-shaking, he will remove another petal and hold it up. "Is this a flower?"

One by one, he will remove each of the petals, establishing that it is not, in fact, a flower. Before holding the denuded stalk of the flower he will ask, "Is this a flower? No? Of course not! It is only a flower when it has all its petals. It exists only dependent on its parts. There is no flowerness that remains after the parts have been separated. It is the same with you and me. We have to get over this idea that there is some separate, independent, self-existent 'me' which has all kinds of characteristics. A 'me' that exists independent of its parts. Such a thing doesn't exist. Couldn't exist. Never has existed. We are all merely dependent arisings."

Les's dharma teachings in general, and those on dependent arising in particular, were to assume special significance after my return to Perth from New York. Despite the shock of the September 11 experience, I had returned with high expectations that my third novel, *Expiry Date*, would be bought by a US publisher. Both my agent and editor in London were enthusiastic about it, as was my New York agent. The subject certainly felt right for the time. I had a good feeling about the book, it seemed so appropriate given the rapidly growing interest in life sciences.

Set in the world of biotechnology, the central "What if?" question in *Expiry Date* was, What if our rate of aging could be slowed down by twenty percent to thirty percent? What if we could effortlessly add on an extra thirty years to our expected life span?

The search for the elixir of life is as old as mankind, but with all the scientific breakthroughs since the Human Genome Project, concepts which have only ever existed in fiction are now becoming a real possibility. Hoping that all this would strike a chord with New York book editors, I was surprised by the length of time everything seemed to be taking. I'd always been led to believe that things in New York happened much more quickly than in London. And as used to the waiting game as I was, I became by turns disappointed, then resigned when one week followed another and still I'd heard nothing from my agent.

I immersed myself in my PR work, and also in putting the finishing touches to the draft of a new story I was writing, *The Evil Within*. This time, the context for the thriller was growth hormones in meat. How, I wonder, is it possible for human beings to ingest large quantities of drug-treated animal flesh without the hormones having an effect on them too? Surely the hormones must have an impact further up the food chain?

A little research quickly revealed this to be the case. Even more shocking was the discovery that one of America's most widely used growth hormones is banned in Europe, where it is considered to be carcinogenic.

A fictitious fast-food chain, Texas Sheriff, provided the context for *The Evil Within*. Drawing on all the lessons I'd learned from my first three novels, I crafted a contemporary thriller which I hoped would find broad resonance on both sides of the Atlantic. And while still waiting on developments in New York, I was particularly pleased when my London agent, to whom I'd sent a draft of *The Evil Within*, responded with enthusiasm.

Rediscovering the First Noble Truth

For my birthday in February 2002, Janmarie took me away to the luxurious Empire retreat in Margaret River. It was wonderfully relaxing—we spent several days touring the local wineries and eating in their casually elegant restaurants. At dusk we'd set out into the nearby bush, watching the dust-red backs of the kangaroos as they loped into the darkness, or walking along the beach, savoring the sand beneath our bare feet as the breakers foamed about our ankles.

It was late in the evening, on the day we drove back to Perth, that I received a sharp reminder of the First Noble Truth. An email from New York was waiting for me, telling me that there'd been several rejections of *Expiry Date*, and that with the New York publishing world still coming to grips with the aftershock of September 11, the time wasn't right to continue marketing the story. In short, there wasn't going to be a

US sale any time soon. Which meant there wouldn't be even the possibility of a Hollywood deal and the momentum that would provide. Things in New York were becalmed, and there was nothing, it seemed, that I could do about it.

But that was only the start. A far more lethal fax had come through from London. My editor had just read the first draft of *The Evil Within* and, unlike my previous work, couldn't find anything in it to recommend it. She roundly criticized the characters and seemed to find the plot beyond redemption. She went on to say that recent sales of my books had been disappointing and, in short, suggested that I find myself another publisher.

From that single communication I knew the plug had been well and truly pulled on my thriller-writing career. So much for the publisher's much-vaunted "long-term approach." So much for all the brand-building support I would be given as an up-and-coming writer. The paperback of my second book had barely been published, and I'd already been fired.

This shocking news was all the more bewildering in light of the most recent conversation I'd had with my editor, just a few months before, when she'd not only assured me that sales of my books were "solid," she'd gone on to explain that my publishers were so confident of *Expiry Date* they were planning to launch it as a stand-alone title, rather than in conjunction with the paperback of *Pure Deception*. How could the world have changed so much in such a short time? Why hadn't my agent and I been told about it?

My instant reaction was to feel bitter and betrayed. Such a comprehensive reversal of position was utterly confusing. More than that, as soon as I read the fax I knew there would be little further promotion of my books. Worst of all, despite the excitement surrounding *Expiry Date*, the novel was destined to be stillborn. There would be no advertising. No reviews. No promotion of any kind. Chances were, very few people would ever discover its existence. In the event, things turned out worse than I imagined. Without so much as an email to explain, later that year the hardback edition was quietly dropped, so that *Expiry Date* slipped into the book trade in large paperback format, virtually unnoticed.

Loyal readers who contacted me via my website provided a much-appreciated source of encouragement with their enthusiastic reception when they read *Expiry Date*, having hunted down copies. But the competitive reality of the book trade is such that unless a new author's books are strongly promoted, they will never be heard above the noise of established bestsellers. Without a committed publisher and an effective marketing campaign, an author is destined to remain a voice in the wilderness.

An alternative reality

In coming to terms with all this, I could hardly fail to recognize that two very different interpretations could be applied to what was happening. If I wished, I could see this reversal as a personal catastrophe, evidence that my chosen career had ended in spectacular failure. I could see it as bad luck, duplicity, the slump effect on the book trade caused by September 11, plus a host of other things.

Or I could regard it as the perfectly normal state of affairs in samsara, devoid of any significance beyond that which I chose to give it.

Buddha's First Noble Truth, that the nature of samsara is dissatisfaction, was a teaching I had never been more sure of! And while it was easy to lay the blame for my suffering on all kinds of external circumstances, the real cause, as Buddha taught in his Second Noble Truth, was my own attachment.

With true Western superstition, I had set out to reshape my external world, believing that my happiness depended on it. Rather than getting a pair of shoes, I had attempted to cover the world with leather. Of course I hadn't succeeded. Even achieving my hard-earned goal of becoming a published novelist hadn't brought me the happiness I'd expected. Quickly, and without any conscious thought on my part, "I will be happy when I become a published novelist" had somehow transmuted into "I will be happy when I become a bestseller." Doubtless, if I had become a bestseller, I would have come to believe that I couldn't feel *really* happy until I occupied the #1 slot, *and* cracked the US market, *and* my books became major Hollywood movies, *and* . . . *and* . . . *and* . . . !

The resentment I felt at having the rug pulled out from under me only showed how much I still believed in the same deluded recipe for happiness. Surely I would have learned my lesson? How many more samsaric flops did it require for me to realize that the cause of my problems wasn't the ingredients I was working with, but the recipe itself?

At least I had some mental tools which now turned out to be extraordinarily powerful in helping me through my disappointment, the most important among them being dependent arising. Recollecting that no event has any intrinsic meaning, that its significance is purely a product of one's own interpretation, I knew that I didn't have to interpret what had happened as a major career disaster, or deep personal failure, or the cause for endless and undiluted misery. I could interpret it any damn way I chose. I could feel relief at no longer having to deal with people in London whose fickleness had been evident from the very start. I could take pleasure in breaking free from the isolation which novel-writing imposed. Given the colossal egotism of some of the people I'd found myself dealing with, I could interpret all this as good riddance.

Quite apart from which, who was this "I" that I was so concerned about? What was this stand-alone, self-existing entity whose feelings needed to be so protected? What was the writing career that seemed to matter so much if not the projection of a projection, different from anyone else's projection and of considerably less interest to them.

Get real! Lighten up! Start making those shoes!

Some while after the fax from my publishers, I discussed my position with my Vajra guru and head of the Tibetan Buddhist Society, Geshe Loden. Should I bother to think about writing ideas in the future, I asked, or forget the whole publishing business?

I knew that if he thought I was wasting my time, he'd tell me to focus on other activities. And I believe his judgment to be informed by far more than normal worldly capabilities. His verbal reply was typically low-key—if I enjoyed writing, he said, by all means continue thinking of new ideas.

But it was the nonverbal message I sensed as I sat with him that made the greatest impact. A heartfelt understanding that whether I wrote another book or not *really didn't matter*. What did matter was much more profound and expansive. Why tie myself up in knots over the fleeting events of a single mindstream during one particular lifetime? Surely there was a bigger picture of more importance? A vision that looked beyond the transient concerns of the moment to a wider horizon? Which, instead of being caught up with a false sense of Self, also encompassed the well-being of all others?

I could make myself miserable in the confines of my sesame seed-size Self, or I could relax into a much truer recognition of reality: boundless, pristine, interconnected, blissful.

One story, two endings

My thrillers, true to genre, always end on an up. Harm will certainly befall the good guys. There's no way that the hero and heroine, faced with increasingly threatening odds, will emerge unscathed. But ultimately there is a moral victory. Good triumphs over evil. The wicked are wished "hasta la vista, baby." We can go to sleep at night content in the certain knowledge that however much the villains might dominate the proceedings during the course of the drama, somehow, in the end, they will have their comeuppance.

Of course, real life is not as tidy as that. In relating my own experiences, I wish I could end this story with a last-ditch quirk of fate which saw victory snatched from the frothing and blood-flecked jaws of defeat. Alas, there has been no late-night phone call from the New York editor, who happened to find a dog-eared copy of one of my books stuffed into the seat pocket in front of him on the plane, and who couldn't go to sleep until clinching a seven-figure deal. Ditto the Hollywood producer searching for a dazzling contemporary thriller, who voraciously consumed one of my stories in a single sitting. Don't worry—my samsaric fantasies are every bit as vivid as the next person's!

From a covering-the-world-with-leather point of view this is a story that ends on a downer. But to leave it there would be to completely miss the point. Because looking at things from a making-a-pair-of-shoes perspective, a somewhat different picture emerges.

Before I studied the Dharma, I was condemned to live according to the rules of superstitious materialism. Although my default mode remains this way, at least now I have some recognition that what's out there doesn't equal what is within. That, alone, marks a profound change.

There is also the wonderful knowledge of dependent arising. The discovery that you are making the whole thing up—yourself, your dreams, your reputation, your life—can be a shocking experience for some. For someone like me, predisposed to take myself too seriously for my own happiness, it can come as a huge relief. So many of the pressures and expectations we beat ourselves up about arise directly from our own flawed understanding of the way that things exist. Correct this understanding, even to a small extent, and life immediately becomes gentler, more expansive.

The shoes I am fashioning for myself are still thin and let in the prickles. But I know that through mindfulness, bodhichitta, and dependent arising, those shoes are getting thicker and more robust.

And what is more important? To seek a success which will be constantly at the whim of events beyond one's control? Or to progress towards a blissful state which is beyond threat because it is founded on a more accurate understanding of reality?

10. Following a Teacher

*The fulfillment of a seeker's higher aspirations is not so much
dependent on accumulating knowledge as on overcoming mental
obstacles and gaining insight into the truth in oneself. For this,
the guidance of an experienced teacher is a practical necessity.*

——————   LOBSANG P. LHALUNGA, *The Life of Milarepa*   ——————

A T THE END of formal presentations to clients, in my role as
corporate communications advisor, I usually have a section called "Next Steps." If the client concurs with my
analysis of their needs, agrees with my plan of action, and is
not overly alarmed by my proposed fee, then we discuss what
should happen next.

"Next Steps" usually means "First Steps." Having agreed on
the direction we should be taking, we decide on how we should
start out on the journey.

In understanding the Dharma, our first step is clearly identified as finding a suitable teacher. For this reason, Lam Rim
teachings traditionally emphasize this right at the start. I, however, have kept this subject until the end. Why? Because many
of us in the West have a well-founded suspicion of anything
that smacks of cults, cranks, and crooks, particularly when

applied to personal development. We have seen too many cult leaders who are multiple Rolls-Royce owners, or who lead their followers to mass suicide in the South American jungle, or self-immolation in Waco. The idea of entrusting anyone with something as important as our minds is not something we would consider without knowing exactly what we are letting ourselves in for.

Buddhism agrees. There are carefully formulated criteria to be considered when choosing a potential teacher, and we are cautioned to scrutinize anyone we might be considering as a guru for anything up to twelve years before making any commitment. This is not an impulse purchase. Our objective is altogether too important to waste our time with phonies or charlatans. But nor should we be under any illusion that without a suitable teacher our progress will be anything other than extremely limited. In the words of Geshe Loden, "We should be careful not to hand the string attached to this ring through our nose to just anybody and ensure that we entrust ourselves to a fully qualified guru with the ten qualities."

The word "guru" can be translated as "spiritual friend." But because "guru" has acquired so many negative connotations, I prefer the word "teacher" which, in its best sense, is an accurate description of the purpose to be fulfilled.

Most of us can remember at least one teacher from our schooldays who made a real and positive difference to us. Someone who awakened our interest in literature, or science or history or sports. Someone we looked up to, and perhaps wanted to emulate, part teacher, part friend, part psychologist, who knew exactly how to engage our interest and motivate us to strive extra hard to achieve peak performance. This is the role of the teacher in Buddhism.

Since Buddhism is a practice-based psychology, it is useful to have someone to coach us in mastering every action of body, speech, and mind. But we will also benefit from working with someone who knows us well enough to understand our own particular hang-ups and limitations, who will encourage us when we fall into a depression, guide us through obstacles when we face them—someone, in short, who can transmit the Buddha's teachings in a way that will talk to us as individuals. To quote Sakya Pandita:

> Though the sun's rays are very hot,
> There will be no fire without a lens;
> Likewise the blessings of the Buddhas
> Cannot be received without a guru.

Book learning is all very well and has an important part in our inner journey. But it has its limitations. Aspiring pianists might work out for themselves how to play "Twinkle, Twinkle Little Star" without the benefit of a piano teacher, but how about a piano concerto by Mozart or a Chopin scherzo? Rudimentary concepts can be absorbed with ease, but what about more complex ones? And what if we form a mistaken understanding of a core but subtle teaching early on, only to discover that this creates limitations which we have to review much later on? We cannot become engineers or surgeons or architects without teachers—how can we become Buddhas without them?

Sutra and tantra

The Lam Rim teachings in this book belong to the sutra tradition of Tibetan Buddhism. For students with a good understanding of the Lam Rim, and who are fortunate to have received appropriate initiations, there is also a tantra tradition, where the role of the teacher becomes more significant still.

On this point I'd like to refer to the advertisements for so-called tantric sex which frequently appear in New Age magazines. "So you study tantra, do you?" friends will sometimes inquire with knowing smiles. "What exactly goes on at those weekend retreats?"

It's worth saying, for the record, that nothing to do with the tantric sex you see advertised has any connection to Tibetan Buddhism. It may very well purport to. Its advocates may promise to make sex sacred—whatever that's supposed to mean. But the idea that ordinary people can move towards enlightenment by having sex is beguiling, attachment-based nonsense. Tantric sex workshops may very well improve your love life, but they have nothing to do with mental development, and in believing that they do one risks becoming only more deluded!

The real tantra tradition in Tibetan Buddhism goes by a number of synonyms, one of which is "secret." The intense privacy surrounding its practice is strictly observed, which is why you would never see it advertised in a magazine. The reason for this secrecy has a lot to do with ensuring that initiates receive correct teachings regarding highly complex visualizations and chants. None of this, however, involves taking your clothes off!

The qualities of a teacher

The qualities to be sought in a perfect teacher have been long established. According to Maitreya's *Ornament for the Maha-*

yana Sutras, the first thing we should look for is "pure morality." I am always amazed by the naivete of some enthusiastic
truth-searchers who join ashrams or other communities run
by charismatic frauds who predictably make off with their followers' money, and sometimes their girlfriends, to resurface
in other parts of the world with fresh identities. One famous
televangelist used to seduce his female followers with the dis-
ingenuous line "Help the shepherd help the sheep." The verse
doesn't appear anywhere in the Bible, but it was enough justi-
fication for some devotees to swoon into his arms.

Part of ensuring that potential teachers "walk the talk" is
to judge their meditation credentials. While we have no way
of knowing what's going on in a teacher's head at any one
moment, their behavior out of formal meditation practice
should give us some clues. Does he or she seem to be a person
whose mind is "pacified and undistracted through the practice
of meditation"? If a teacher comes across as being touchy, con-
ceited, disorganized, or unable to see a task through, what does
that tell us about their aptitude for single-pointed concentration, or their grasp of dependent arising?

In addition to the qualities already mentioned, it goes
almost without saying that our chosen teacher should not
only be knowledgeable about the Dharma, but also a skilled
and enthusiastic communicator. During my years exploring
Buddhism I've gone to a number of lectures outside my regular dharma centers, and have been struck by the wide variety
of approaches to teaching. Some of this reflects the different
schools within Tibetan Buddhism, which each have their own
points of emphasis. But to a much greater extent the variation
reflects the individuals themselves, their diverse personalities,
and their different stages on the path to enlightenment.

As a fifteen-year-old schoolboy I remember the headmaster proudly announcing to the first school assembly of the year that the staff had been joined by Dr. Matthews, who would head up the Mathematics Department. The only Ph.D. on the staff, Dr. Matthews was a tall, ascetic-looking man who had studied at a variety of Ivy League universities and was widely regarded as a mathematical genius.

Later in the day my class was told he would be taking us for math that year. We were a bright but restless group with some of that year's star pupils; providing Dr. Matthews could maintain discipline, great things were expected of us.

From the very beginning, Dr. Matthews's teaching methods were a cause of unhappiness. He skated over each subject in the curriculum with such speed that we hadn't even grasped quadratic equations before he was onto advanced calculus. He would digress from any given topic into related areas he found more interesting—he understood the big picture, how everything fit together, but most of us were still struggling with the building blocks. Worst of all, when we tried to explain the difficulties we were having, he just couldn't see our problem.

At the end-of-year Parents and Teachers Association meeting there were a lot of anxious faces. Pupil discontent was one thing, but the sweep of fail grades was quite another; the mothers and dads demanded that something be done.

The following year, our first of public exams, Mr. Fourie was appointed as our math teacher. Unlike Dr. Matthews, he was not thought to possess any great intellect, and he had no university degree, only a teaching diploma. But what he did have was an understanding of the problems we faced, because he had faced them too. He knew exactly why we were getting stuck on things, having once gotten stuck on them himself. Not only did he show us how to overcome the hurdles, he rebuilt our confidence—if Mr. Fourie could crack math, then so could we.

At the hearts of the dharma centers spreading through the West there are many Dr. Matthews and Mr. Fouries. All of them serve their purpose. (As it happens, Dr. Matthews found his way into the local university where he was much admired—he'd found his level.) I have gone to lectures by visiting high-ranking lamas and come away disappointed and uninspired. By contrast, a casual conversation with a Buddhist friend can often stimulate a line of thought that I return to for days.

What can't be emphasized enough is to find a teacher whom you can relate to, who speaks to you where you are at this moment, and to take your time observing him or her closely. Our enlightenment, and the enlightenment of others, is the biggest project of our lives. It is something we need to get right.

The qualities of a student

The qualities of a student have also been long established in Buddhism. They include the checklist you might expect—concentration, application, respect for your teacher and the Dharma. But they also include the quality of having a questioning attitude, specifically an atttitude ensuring that the teachings you receive are in accordance with the established Dharma.

One of the most common criticisms of Buddhism I come across is the idea that in following a particular teacher, practitioners are somehow allowing themselves to become brainwashed. From the outside, it's easy to see why people might think that practitioners fall under the spell of their guru, given their efforts to carry out instructions.

But as this teaching shows, there is no room for passivity on the part of a student. This is not a one-way process, like watching TV. Students are, instead, engaged in a dynamic activity in which we are constantly assessing and questioning the teachings, thinking about how they apply to our lives. In following a teacher, dharma students are not abdicating responsibility for their future to someone else. Quite the opposite. Just as the occupants of a prisoner-of-war camp might value the advice of a tunnel engineer, or a group of lost explorers would have much to learn from a navigation expert, the actual business of escaping from samsara is something we need to do for ourselves—and, of course, for others.

Relying on our teacher

As Westerners living in consumerist times, we are accustomed to upgrading our cars, replacing our furniture, and improving our jobs every few years. Some people apply this same principle to their romantic partners. Whatever we have, we know there is a better version to be found. Even if we own a top of the line car of our favorite make, it will only take a few years for ours to become the "old model."

It is important to drop this attitude when we accept someone as our teacher. Being a dharma dilettante is not an option if we are serious about making progress. Big-name lamas may visit our country offering amazing initiations. We may have an opportunity to hear teachings from the Dalai Lama himself. While these may be useful, we shouldn't allow ourselves to be distracted too much from our main relationship with our teacher. Flitting from one lama to the next, convinced that each one holds secret wisdom superior to the last, is to fall into the trap of believing your development is dependent on what's out there. Rather, it is your own mind that requires the work, and relying on a teacher who knows your personal hang-ups and can help you surmount them is of far greater value than seeking miraculous solutions from other lamas, however high ranking.

In the words of Geshe Potawa:

> Do not accept many gurus without analyzing,
> But once accepting him, respect your teacher.
> Then naturally in the future you will not lack a teacher.
> Karma created will not be fruitless!

As well as cultivating a correct attitude of respect towards one's teacher, we are also encouraged to devote ourselves by actions. Specifically, these include offering material things, paying respect/doing service, and practicing as our teacher instructs. Of these three, the most important is to practice as our teacher instructs.

As in all things, Buddhism encourages us to use wisdom in our relationship with our teacher. When making material offerings to our teacher, it's important to provide something that's appropriate. Before I first met my own Vajra guru, Geshe Loden, I inquired what sort of gift I should give him. I was advised that whatever I decided on, I should try to get the highest quality item of its kind. I was also told that Geshe-la recycles all his gifts. Sure enough, having arrived with a box of Belgian chocolates, I emerged with a tin of gourmet biscuits!

216 · *Buddhism for Busy People*

While the quality of one's gift says something about one's intentions, it's also important to make offerings, however modest, with a willing heart. There is a wonderful story about how Geshe-la was offered a cup of tea by a distracted student one day, but turned down the offer. Moments later another student appeared in the room and suggested he make a cup of tea. This time Geshe-la accepted.

"Why didn't you say you wanted a cup when I offered it?" asked the first student.

"Because you didn't really mean it!" he replied.

Following the instructions of our teacher

What if our teacher suggests we should start trying to convert our friends to Buddhism? What if he tells us to shave our heads and adopt a more saintly demeanor? As it says in the *Vinaya Sutra*, "If it does not conform with the Dharma, do the opposite!"

While the cultivation of faith in our teacher is important, as already noted, it should never be blind faith, nor should it be practiced at the expense of wisdom. Lama Yeshe was well known among those who heard him teach for advising students to "check up." It was one of his most-used catch phrases.

While we should check up on a teacher's instructions, we should also check up on our minds, which are the source of the qualities we project. In times of difficulty in particular we need to ask ourselves, How much of this problematic projection is my teacher, and how much of it is me?

The advantages of a teacher

While the advantages of relying on a teacher should be apparent from a common-sense perspective, what of the karmic implications?

Having chosen a teacher, we are told that by making a lifelong commitment to our teacher we are creating the karmic causes for the flowering of enormous benefits in our future mindstream. For starters, we are creating the cause to meet a good teacher in our future lives. Similarly, by cultivating respect for him we will not fall into the lower realms, but move rapidly towards achieving all our aims, both worldly objectives as well as enlightenment.

The *Essence of the Nectar Graduated Path* says:

> In brief, by devotion to the guru, for the present
> You will be free from unfavorable states and
> Attain the higher states of humans and gods.
> Ultimately all the suffering of cyclic existence will
> be ended
> And you will achieve the supreme excellent state.

By breaking our commitment to our teacher, however, not only do we create the causes to lack such a guide in the future, we also seriously imperil our future. In particular, by bad-mouthing the person we once took as our teacher we create the causes for immense damage to our progress, condemning ourselves to countless lifetimes in lower realms where mental development isn't even a possibility.

Our teacher: The foundation of all realizations

Cultivating respect for and faith in another person seems a curiously old-fashioned idea in the early twenty-first century. We do not live in a society where these values are greatly honored—by contrast, cynicism and doubt can seem far more effective tools for survival. For this reason, talk of serving one's teacher can sound strange, even foreign. That kind of thing might work in subservient cultures like Tibet, we might think, but we in the West have a rather more advanced approach to civil liberties and freedom of expression. Not for us, terrifying people into submission!

But as travelers on a path of inner transformation we need to recognize that we wouldn't know of the existence of this path, let alone how to progress most swiftly along it, were it not for our teachers.

As the texts say, Buddhas cannot remove the sufferings of ordinary beings by the touch of their hand, or wash away sins with water. The way that they can most benefit the fortunate is by showing them the Dharma and guiding their practice. Geshe Loden points out, "If we look to see who is undertaking such activity today, we find that it is none other than holy Gurus . . . Saying that a Guru is an ordinary person implies that Buddhas need the help of ordinary people to guide others in practicing the Dharma. This would be like saying that a wealthy person requires the help of a beggar to make a purchase."

The way we think about our teacher has a lot less to do with our teacher than it does with our mind. As we've already seen in the chapter on dependent arising, there is nothing objective about external reality; rather, it is a projection of our mind. If we find ourselves becoming disenchanted with our teacher, perhaps it's not the teacher that needs to be changed—perhaps it is our mind.

The critical importance of our teacher in our future destiny is summed up in a marvelous story about Naropa, a luminary of the Mahayana tradition, and his equally famous student Marpa. Towards the end of their time together, while Marpa was sleeping one night, Naropa, who was an extremely accomplished yogi, projected a particular manifestation of Buddha in the sky, complete with spectacular retinue. Next he woke up Marpa, telling him that the Buddha was in the sky.

Seeing that this was true, Marpa was amazed. Naropa then tested his student by asking, "Will you prostrate to me first, or the Buddha?"

Prostrating is a traditional way of marking respect in the Tibetan monastic tradition.

Marpa decided to prostrate to the Buddha on the basis that he might only get to see him this once, while he could see Naropa any time he liked. But no sooner had he done so than Naropa pointed out:

> Prior to the Guru, there is not even the name "Buddha."
> Also, all the Buddhas of a thousand eons arise from Gurus.

Without a teacher there is no Dharma. We have no possibility of escaping samsara. Even coping with our day-to-day lives becomes very much harder. Therefore, in setting out to follow the Buddhist path, finding a satisfactory teacher is of primary importance.

While dharma centers are increasingly opening up in Western cities, finding a teacher we can relate to, and who represents the pure lineage, is not always easy. As in all things, Buddhism encourages us to take this important step with common sense and caution. Seeking out a celebrity guru should not be our objective. Of far greater importance is the wisdom of a compassionate heart.

When the pupil is ready . . .

You've probably heard that old adage "when the pupil is ready, the teacher will appear." It certainly has proven true for me, although the reality is probably more along the lines that the teacher was always there, I just needed to want to find him.

Talking to other Buddhists, I've found my experience reflects theirs. And apart from the surprising availability of a teacher when really needed, I've come across another interesting phenomenon. After classes, I find when talking to other students about what they understood from the teachings that they often come out with very different interpretations than mine. Not necessarily in conflict with my understanding; more a matter of emphasis. Insights which are highly meaningful to some people don't strike others as being important, and vice versa.

There are stories about not only Buddha, but other great teachers including Jesus' disciple Peter, speaking to large multicultural groups of people, all of whom heard the teacher in their own language. We can take these stories literally. But on an everyday basis, our experience is similar: we may all be receiving the same teachings, but each one of us hears something different.

The relationship between a dharma teacher and his students is certainly no ordinary one. What a student derives from the relationship has as much to do with where that student is on the path and his or her particular needs, as it has to do with the teacher. In this sense, the teacher is less a communicator of ideas than a facilitator who helps us work through the individual obstacles in our particular mindstream.

Our teacher occupies a special place in our lives, different from that held by anyone else. We may be loved by our partners, friends, and relatives, but in our relationships with them can we rely on them to be free of subjectivity and self-interest? A therapist may provide a similar level of objectivity, but it would be unusual for them to have the perspective that sees beyond this particular lifetime and its sesame seed-like preoccupations.

Our teacher, by contrast, is mainly interested in helping us achieve lasting happiness so that we, in turn, can give this happiness to others. He brings to our relationship a panorama of dazzling possibility, and in so doing his kindness is one that we can never repay.

Epilogue

HAT DOES IT TAKE to be happy? To return to our original starting point, Lam Rim teachings provide explicit instructions that are simple, direct, and illuminating, if not always easy to practice. In summary, true happiness arises when we are able to change our minds rather than the world around us, when we loosen the bonds of self-focus enough to care more for others. It follows the recognition that all phenomena, ourselves included, exist merely as dependent arisings. Renunciation, bodhichitta, and special wisdom, the lotus, moon, and sun—these give direction to the transcendent bliss which is the destiny of each one of us.

But long before we get even close to this, our ultimate goal, by living mindfully as we are guided by a skillful teacher, and by practicing compassion, little by little we discover that we aren't who we thought we were at all. We can let go of our narrow and restricting self-beliefs. We can dump our sesame seed-size preoccupations. We become aware of our role in a very much more panoramic drama, of our truly dazzling opportunity, way beyond the confines of the being we usually think of as "me."

For my own part, even though my own steps along the dharma path have been few and tentative, I wouldn't like to imagine life without these precious teachings. Through meditation I access a reservoir of calm and objectivity from which I benefit each day. Dependent arising has already made me more resilient in the face of personal upset. Bodhichitta is helping me open my heart.

While I certainly wouldn't hold myself up as some kind of bodhisattva, it has been my enormous privilege to meet people who are. There can be no higher tribute to a practice-based tradition than leaders such as the Dalai Lama; my own Vajra guru, Geshe Loden; my teacher Les Sheehy; and Western nun Tenzin Palmo, to name but a few. These beings live with a radiant immediacy and a compassion which is observable, sometimes palpable—and can be quite overwhelming.

A new edition, a new journey

I wrote the first edition of *Buddhism for Busy People* in 2003 inspired by, more than anyone, my teacher Les, who has a very direct, humorous, and engaging way of presenting the Dharma. My hope was that if I could write a book version of the way Les teaches, I would be creating an introduction to Buddhism that would be truly different from the many introductory texts already available. I was delighted when the publishing team at Allen & Unwin agreed.

From the beginning, *Buddhism for Busy People* was a refreshingly different publishing experience. To start with, my publisher is herself a Tibetan Buddhist, which meant that both of us brought to the project an awareness that we had the potential to achieve a lot more than book sales alone. What's more, as the launch date of November, 2004 came and went, I had none of the concerns I'd felt in the past about what the latest sales data from Bookscan might be. I had already decided to donate all my royalties from the book to charity—I wasn't doing this for the money.

All the same, I was delighted when my publisher phoned, the month after publication, to say that sales had been so strong Allen & Unwin was running a reprint. Bookstores right around the country were reordering and news of the book seemed to be spreading by the most effective form of marketing in the world—word of mouth.

A second reprint was to follow within months before, amazingly, a third, then a fourth. In the meantime, the foreign rights team was also enjoying some success. I could only wonder at the irony when the very first language rights deal was struck with a publisher in—it just seemed unbelievable—China! Further rights deals were secured in countries as diverse as Holland, Russia, and Turkey. And a distributor in the US was signed up.

From a Dharma point of view it seems that *Buddhism for Busy People* has, in itself, proved that if one embarks on a project with the right motivation, and without attachment to a particular outcome, the most wonderful events can unfold.

And on a personal level there is no question that *Buddhism for Busy People* has been the most deeply satisfying publishing experience of my life. I have been both amazed and humbled by the emails I've received from readers through my website, telling me about their response to the book and sharing their personal experiences. I've been truly moved by the many intelligent, articulate readers who have responded in such a profound and heartfelt way.

Inevitably, I've found myself questioning if I have, without realizing it, begun in a new direction. Are there other Dharma-type books I could be writing? Other creative ways I could work to practice that most important generosity of all—the generosity of giving Dharma?

The Buddha's greatest gift

The *Diamond Sutra* tells of an exchange between the Buddha and one of his students, Subhuti:

> The Buddha asked Subhuti, "Does one who has immersed himself in the stream that flows to enlightenment say of himself, 'I have entered the stream'?" Subhuti replied, "No, Buddha. He is called a stream-enterer because he knows he has attained nothing. If the thought, 'I have attained the state of entering the stream' were to occur to him, then he would be clutching to a personality or soul or some idea of a separate self."

It is this, most of all, which is the Buddha's greatest gift. Even if we come to the Dharma looking only for a few tools to help make ourselves happier, we stumble into an altogether different understanding of reality—one in which we are not a wave at all but are simply, gloriously, water. With an intellectual understanding alone, the knowledge of this certainty relieves us of the burden of ourselves, awakening us to a far more expansive consciousness that is boundless, blissful—and right now.

It is my sincere wish that this book has provided some useful tools to help you achieve happiness to reinterpret the way you experience the world, to create calm amid the busyness and, beneath the uncertainties of everyday life, a sense of profound peace. Most of all, I hope the Buddha's teachings have provided at least a glimpse of your own true nature and the radiant transcendence at your heart.

Dedication

By this virtue, may I and all beings without exception
Enjoy vibrant good health, long life, abundance, and
boundless love.
From our hearts may we take refuge in the triple gem,
Generate the peerless mind of bodhichitta,
And realize the ultimate truth of dependent arising.

By practicing mindfulness, bodhichitta, and the six
perfections,
Guided by a teacher of pure lineage,
May we all quickly and easily attain
The supreme great bliss of enlightenment.

Glossary

Attachment   The mistaken belief that an object, person, or situation is a true cause of happiness.

Aversion   The mistaken belief that an object, person, or situation is a true cause of unhappiness.

Bodhichitta   Lit. "the mind of enlightenment." The aspiration to achieve enlightenment to free all living beings from suffering.

Bodhisattva   A person who wishes to attain enlightenment to free all living beings from suffering.

Buddha   Lit. "awakenened one." A fully awakened being who has attained enlightenment.

Dependent arising   The idea that all beings and phenomena depend for their existence on parts, causes, and projection of the mind.

Dharma   The doctrine or teachings of the Buddha.

Enlightenment   A state in which the mind is awakened to its true nature, which is boundless, omniscient, and blissful.

Guru   Spiritual friend.

Karma   Lit. "action" or "deed." Implies "reaction," and the concept of cause and effect.

Lam Rim   The graduated path to enlightenment.

Mantra   Lit. "mind protection." In general practice, a collection of sounds recited in connection with a particular meditation to achieve a particular outcome.

Nirvana   Lit. "to extinguish" the false sense of self. Generally refers to personal liberation from samsara.

Samsara   Mind afflicted by karma and delusion. It is this mind which perpetuates the universal cycle of birth, death, and rebirth by grasping at a false sense of self.

Sangha   The community of Buddhist monks and nuns. In the West the term "lay Sangha" refers to practitioners who have not been ordained.

Tantra   Advanced teachings of Tibetan Buddhism
                    practiced only after initiations.

Thangka   An illustrative wall hanging.

Tulku   A recognized reincarnate lama. One who
                    has voluntarily been reborn to help others
                    to enlightenment.

Further Reading

H.H. The Dalai Lama, *The Path to Enlightenment*. Ithaca, N.Y.: Snow Lion Publications, 1995.

Lama Surya Das, *Awakening the Buddha Within*. New York: Broadway Books, 1997.

Geshe Acharya Thubten Loden, *Path to Enlightenment*. Melbourne: Tushita Publications, 1993.

Vicki Mackenzie, *Reincarnation: The Boy Lama*. Boston: Wisdom Publications, 1996.

Vicki Mackenzie, *Cave in the Snow: Tenzin Palmo's Quest for Enlightenment*. New York: Bloomsbury, 1998.

Vicki Mackenzie, *Why Buddhism?* London: Thorsons, 2003.

Thich Nhat Hanh, *The Heart of Understanding*. Berkeley, Calif.: Parallax Press, 1997.

Tenzin Palmo, *Reflections on a Mountain Lake*. Ithaca, N.Y.: Snow Lion Publications, 2002.

Geshe Michael Roach, *The Diamond Cutter*. New York: Doubleday, 2000.

Shantideva, *The Way of the Bodhisattva*. 2nd ed. Boston: Shambhala, 2006.

Sogyal Rinpoche, *The Tibetan Book of Living and Dying*. Rev. ed. San Francisco: HarperSanFrancisco, 2002.